WOMEN'S IMAGES, MEN'S IMAGINATION

Female characters in Bengali fiction in late nineteenth and early twentieth century

WOMEN'S IMAGES MEN'S IMAGINATION

Female characters in Bengali fiction in late nineteenth and early twentieth century

BANANI MUKHIA

MANOHAR
2002

First published 2002

ISBN 81-7304-410-4

Published by
Ajay Kumar Jain for
Manohar Publishers & Distributors
4753/23 Ansari Road, Daryaganj
New Delhi 110 002

Typeset by
P.K. Goel for
Aditya Prakashan
F 14/65, Model Town II
Delhi 110 009

Printed at
Print Perfect
A 23 Mayapuri, Phase II
New Delhi 110 064

For Harbans

Contents

Preface

This book has been long in coming. Working for it has been a great joy for one born and raised as a Bengali female in a strong Bengali milieu, who took to studying and teaching English literature, was introduced to Panjabi and north Indian social landscape through marital and habitational ties but who still speaks English with a strong Bengali accent and Hindi with profound indifference to its gender sensitivities; she was permitted registration for the doctoral degree in the Department of Sociology, Jamia Millia Islamia, at a stage in her life when the mind is often beset with some anxiety and much relief at the approaching retirement from service. All these myriad experiences have shaped the research, long in gestation, to culminate in this work.

It is the contours of this hybrid cultural and academic map that are reflected in the choice of the theme, its treatment and even the choice of the novels and stories that I selected for analysis. A strong reason for this choice was the fact that these were essentially women-centred stories in which women had been imaged from a great diversity of backgrounds, characters, moods as well as patterns of behaviour, so as to defy the stereotypical woman. It should have been possible to include stories written by women themselves; if I refrained from doing so, a good part of the reason lay in my wish to explore, in a separate comparative endeavour, the imaging of women in male and female representations in fiction. Hopefully, I should be able to initiate that endeavour now.

As a small, perhaps even an unnecessary aid, I am annexing the gists of the novels that have been analysed in some detail; the short stories do not seem to need such abridgement, for the contents become evident in the course of analysis. The translation of cited Bengali passages has been done by me. I should emphasize that this study focuses entirely on the works of Bankimchandra Chattopadhyay, Rabindranath Tagore and Sarat Chandra Chattopadhyay.

The elements comprising my research interest were put in some order by the generosity and help I constantly received from my supervisor Professor Mohini Anjum, herself from a hybrid cultural milieu.

In the early, exploratory stage of the work, when I had to make frequent visits to the National Library, Calcutta, the indefatigable source of inspiration and moral support had been my sister Dr. Alaka Chattopadhyaya and my brother-in-law Prof. Debiprasad Chattopadhyaya. My sadness at their departure is rendered even more intense by the realization that both of them would have been greatly moved to see the book in print.

I remember having often badgered Meenakshi Mukherjee, whose writings had attracted me into the present study, with many of my uncertainties and anxieties. I remain ever so grateful to her for all the help.

I also had the privilege of a long conversation with Michelle Perrot at her lovely Parisian apartment some years ago when I was still hovering at the periphery of the gender problematic while she had immersed herself deeply in it. The perspective that permeates this work owes ever so much to that conversation and subsequent contact with her work which she always passed on to me with an overwhelming generosity. It is this acquaintance that introduced me to the finesse of gender studies, long way off from binary dividing lines. I am extremely grateful to the UGC and the Maison des Sciences de l'Homme, Paris, to have made the visit to France possible.

The British Council and the Charles Wallace (India) Trust gave welcome help to extend the Paris sojourn to London for looking at some of the Manuscripts and Private Papers and 'Tracts'

(European and Vernacular) at the then India Office Library and Records (since rechristened Oriental and India Office Collections). I owe many thanks to them for recognizing that my project was important at least for me and assisting in its completion.

I feel very grateful to Professors R.K. Jain and Shobita Jain for letting me raid their personal collection of books and for discussing several points of sociological theory with me. For exploration of the historical dimensions of the problem I turned to Professor K.N. Panikkar; I am greatly indebted to him for his help. To Professor Leela Dube I would like to extend a very warm 'thank you' for a rewarding discussion of the feminist question.

My children, Sudeep and Neelanjana, did much of the tedious job of transferring the text on to the computer, extracting time out of their own rather pressing preoccupations. My sociologist son-in-law, Suranjan, never failed to spot short-comings in my argument and be critical, if constructive. It feels good to be their mother.

And of course my sisters, both here in Delhi and in Kolkata, and my brother, all of whom virtually stood guard against my lethargy, though they must have realized it was a losing battle for them. Thanks folks, thanks a lot.

Harbans also helped in some ways. He had to.

October 2000 BANANI MUKHIA

CHAPTER 1

Introduction

'Every woman is an occupied territory' is the somewhat flamboyant title of a recent article by Simona Sharoni.[1] Any other metaphor could scarcely be more evocative of the classic feminist perspective, in which the article has been written, than this one drawn straight from the battle ground. It draws the distinctive lines that implicate conquest, subjugation, humiliation of one half of humankind by the other—a phenomenon uniquely universal and timeless. The perspective, however, is inclined to overlook another facet which, too, is implicated in the metaphor; that the battle ground is a contested terrain in which conquest, subjugation and humiliation are, in every moment of their triumph, challenged by resistance, subversion, inversion, at times explicit, at others subtle, but choosing its strategy and site by discretion, and questioning hegemonic stereotypes which are the chief instruments of women's subjugation.

The linear counter-positioning of men and women, one as the exploiter, the other as exploited—reminiscent of the classic Marxist dichotomy between landlords and serfs, capitalists and workers—distinguished the feminist writings in the 1970s to the mid-1980s; since then linearity of the counter-positioning has become considerably shaded by the vision which dissolved binary collectivities and brought into focus the tensions and movement of everyday life in which each individual seeks to create and enlarge space for oneself within the given structure of relationships. The dynamic of this everyday tension does not demolish the structure, certainly not in a short time-stretch, but does nuance the categories of dominance and subjugation. Several scholars engaged in women's studies have, during the late 1980s and since, diluted the earlier stridency of feminism, while retaining the valuable problematic. Michelle Perrot elaborates this innovative perspective thus:

> In its desire to go beyond the 'miserabiliste' language of oppression, subvert the viewpoint of domination, it [recent feminist research] has sought to show that women are present and active, that they have full roles and a coherent culture and their powers are real.[2]

But she is not alone in such reflection. M.Z. Rosaldo and L. Lamphere, too, resonate with a similar perspective:

> . . . women like men are social actors who act in structured ways to achieve desired ends. Although the formal authority structure of society may declare that women are impotent and irrelevant, close attention to women's strategies and motives, to the sort of choices made by women, to the relationships they establish and the ends they achieve indicate that even in situations of overt sex role asymmetry, women have a good deal more power than conventional theorists have assumed. . . . Women's strategies may appear to be deviant and disruptive, yet they are nonetheless important components of the actual processes by which social life proceeds.[3]

Natalie Z. Davis in several of her historical explorations of the gender problematic in early modern France, too, emphasizes the transformation of the image of weak and hysterical women into an effective source of power.[4] Clearly then, a vision of continuum of relationships, though clearly asymmetrical, is being substituted here for a binary counterpositioning, whether of men and women, or of oppressor and oppressed, or of nature and culture. In the following pages I make an attempt to explore and examine the possibility of such a vision being foregrounded in the present context.

If this work appears to hover between several disciplines, especially literature, sociology and history, it is because of the basic assumption that literature or literary characters for that matter could not possibly be treated in isolation. Literature, of course, has been the primary source and has generated the raw material for my research. Such insight as I have been able to incorporate in exploring interpersonal relationships, I owe to sociology. History remains the backdrop inasmuch as women's social roles, their perceptions of themselves and reflections of these in literature, all constitute a phenomenon, embedded in historical space and time that is innately dynamic, undergoing cardinal mutations, sometimes by severe jerks, at others by a slow, almost imperceptible evolution. The aim here is to explore gender relations, but the perspective, as has already been underlined, is not a frozen opposition between men and women. Its adherence to feminist credentials might perhaps be suspect, but its claim as a study of gender relations beyond the binary oppositions may hopefully expect a more amiable response. My central concern has been the creation and enlargement of personal space within the given structure of gender relations, with its singular specificity of subordination of women to male superordinate authority. It is, in other words, an exploration of the relations of power which, by their very nature, are contested and negotiated every moment that human beings come into direct or indirect contact with one another, each using diverse resources and modes of their deployment in the contest.

In the turbulent intellectual milieu of nineteenth-century Bengal, it was the women's question that came to occupy the central space from Raja Rammohun Roy to Ishwarchandra Vidyasagar and beyond.[5] This space was marked by a growing tension between the existential reality of women's abject subjugation to men's authority—enlarged and sanctified as a social norm—and the rising aspirations of the reform movements which predicated general societal advancement upon at least partial emancipation of women—a tension between history's inertia and imagination's soaring momentum.[6]

Originating essentially in an intellectual ambience, the tension inevitably cast its shadows upon the litterateurs of the age. It did not turn them, not the major ones in any case, into active reformers who would change the world through the practice of their craft, but left them as both the mirrors of the world around them and its interpreters. A major facet of their interpretations and reflections of the society in transition was a changing perception of women's place in the familial and, by extension, social space. In turn the core of literature itself underwent significant mutations as its practice proliferated in the form of new journals and magazines, some of them edited by women themselves, and a new genre of literary text began to gather shape, a genre given to the cause of what has in the past couple of decades come to be identified as women's liberation.[7] In certain writings, in fiction in particular, woman-oriented themes or treatment of female protagonists playing pivotal roles in moving the story forward became less and less unfamiliar to the reading public.

There has been of late a spurt in secondary analyses of the problematic of the portrayal of women in nineteenth-century Bengali literature, some of the authors proclaiming 'powerful' or 'unconventional' female characters as trail blazers of the women's march to modernization.[8]

The present exploration has essentially a socio-psychological setting as its backdrop. It would perhaps be a fair assumption that society always has much to do with constructing psychological matrices of human beings, besides the genetic specificities of each individual's personality formation. Under the strain of the social order which assigned them an inferior location, women appear to be much more predisposed to becoming victims of psychological tension and trauma in shaping their personality than men. Role-playing and role-distancing in this context become all the more significant as role-playing is essentially a normative concept whereas role-distancing carries with it the seeds of unconventionality and often leads to role conflicts.[9] Being enmeshed in some sort of a conflict involving their role duties, women here and there opted for what they conceived was their universal duty, thus creating convoluted and piquant situations in the sphere of interpersonal relationships. The perceived tradition of Indian society has amounted to dissuading women from an assertion of independence, and this perception has transcended other social barriers of class, caste, community, etc. For women the greatest virtue lay in their capacity to submerge their individual identity in the identity of the family; at least that is the socially (i.e. patriarchally) constructed image. Here the endeavour is to contextualize women in the family and its multifaceted relationship with each member, severally and collectively—a study of the representation of interpersonal relationships in the context of the family. In the Indian context in particular, the concept of *Purush/Prakriti* is a principle which is not located in a counterpositioning; instead it strengthens the image of a complementary relationship which also implicates mutual tension.

Power has always been associated with men; it is their historically, culturally and even biologically ordained prerogative. This sort of institutionalized power could be justifiably referred to as authority,[10] whereas

> the exercise of power by women is often seen as manipulative, disruptive, illegitimate or unimportant. But it is necessary to remember that while authority legitimates the use of power, it does not exhaust it, and actual methods of giving rewards, controlling information, exerting pressure, and shaping events may be available to women as well as to men.[11]

Women's power could be defined as *unassigned* or *personal power* which one derives out of an implicit acceptance of an 'individual's right to make decision about particular aspect of social life'.[12] Once again, women's relation with power can be seen first and foremost in language.

> Power is, like many other terms, polysemic. In the singular it has a political connotation and tends to suggest the central, cardinal figure of the state generally accepted as being masculine. In the plural it breaks down into many fragments, which are equated with diffuse, peripheral influences, of which women have a large share.[13]

This is how I intend to deal with the question of feminine power, not in absolute terms, not in its masculine incarnation but how even peripheral influences lend vigour to women's sense of identity, of their personal worth. This sense of identity or personal worth, their self-assertion, sometimes muted, at others overtly articulated, took a definite form, a form of protest, denial, resistance. The eloquence of silence as resistance can be very moving, depending on the context, and mute non-cooperation could be a strong weapon in women's armoury.

Since our study is primarily concerned with the representation of women in Bengali fiction, it should be in order, to examine the status of women and the roles they played in shaping individual and familial profiles in this crucial period of flux. A look at the women and their changing status in their family and society best makes sense in the context of the early reform movements and their implications in moulding male attitudes towards the ills besetting the lives of women. If the following bare outline of the history of the period does not bring forth any unknown fact or uncover a concealed image, it would at least focus on the empirical reality that shaped, and shed light on the social concerns of the authors we are examining. The reform movements and reformist zeal of the leading lights of this period seem to have been characterized by two distinct feelings—an all pervasive sense of shame and inferiority; and a sense of loss, of missed opportunities.

Raja Rammohun Roy, and the subsequent reformers perceived the treatment of women as a national shame. Women were being burnt alive on their husbands' funeral pyres. Women of all ages and the widows, including child widows, were being subjected to a life of utmost rigour often amounting to cruelty. The early reformers were face to face with the duality of standards—one for men and the other for women—practised in orthodox society. In his pamphlet against sati, Raja Rammohun Roy wrote,

> At marriage the wife is recognised as half of her husband, but in after conduct they [*sic*] are treated worse than inferior animals. For, the woman is employed to do the work of a slave in the house . . . to clean the place . . . to scour the dishes, wash the floor, to cook night and day, to prepare and serve food for her husband, father [*sic*], mother-in-law, brothers-in-law and friends and connections.[14]

Gradual exposure to Western philosophy, liberal thinking and practices, particularly the question of women's emancipation as it was discussed in Europe made these pioneers acutely aware of the weaknesses in their own social system. Out of this awareness grew the feeling of shame, at being compared unfavourably with other civilizations, at Indians being regarded with 'contempt and pity . . . by all civilized nations on the surface of the globe'.[15] This sense of shame, again, prompted them to look deeply into their own religious and cultural traditions and seek out the solution to the unhappy situation prevalent in society and ways and means to ameliorate the lot of the unfortunate women.

The early reformers, Rammohun Roy and Ishwarchandra Vidyasagar, looked at women primarily as a collective identity—the satis and the widows. First they tried to strike at the roots of the misery that was the women's lot, and gradually to secure for them an elevated status in society. It was only later on, with the Brahmo reformers and educators and some Hindu social leaders, that the process of viewing women's questions as distinctive problems faced by human individuals started; as a result the question of freedom of movement, freedom from *purdah*, freedom of social interaction with the members of the opposite sex and freedom to ascertain and question the conjugal rights and responsibilities arose. Whereas both Rammohun and Vidyasagar made an all out effort to obliterate the 'national shame' by initiating the process of abolishing *satidaha* and paving the way for widow remarriage, the latter day reformers on their part tried to redefine the roles of women in the family and in society, though the family still set the limits of their freedom.

With Rammohun's crusade against sati started the reform movement in nineteenth-century Bengal which gradually spread to other areas of public consciousness, including women's issues. Rammohun concerned himself with other issues like polygamy, women's property rights, etc. For abolition of sati, Rammohun realized, legal intervention was as necessary as the awakening of public conscience against this inhuman practice. The British administration in the initial stage following the policy of non-interference in the social and religious affairs of the 'natives' was reluctant to intervene. 'Roy's mobilization of Hindu thought against the system of "sati" created the necessary public opinion to enable the government, which was also under pressure from missionaries on this issue to make the practice a criminal offence in 1829.'[16] That legislation alone is never potent enough to halt the perpetuation of 'social evils' was so amply demonstrated in the Roop Kanwar episode of 1987. (In that year a young, married woman in Rajasthan, suddenly widowed, committed sati on her husband's funeral pyre, even as law forbids the act.) Nobody had realized the truth of it more profoundly than Vidyasagar who had dedicated half his life towards making widow remarriage a practical proposition. In the present discourse remarriage of the widows is a much more relevant and compelling force to deal with. The practice of sati had ceased to be a palpable problem by the end of the nineteenth century. Widow remarriage on the other hand was a question with a perpetual controversy raging around it. In literature as in the broader canvas of society it has always remained an open ended question—whether to support the issue or not—and in the end Vidyasagar stood alone amidst his shattered dreams, a bitter and disillusioned man. After a long and sustained effort on his part the bill legalizing the marriage of Hindu widows was passed in 1856.

> But neither the Act of 1856, nor the lifelong effort of Vidyasagar to carry it to practice, could mitigate much of the conventional hostility of Hindu society to widow-marriage. In the main, the Act remained a dead letter since widow marriages remained exceptional in the higher castes.[17]

He had to spend a fortune to see his life's most important mission translated into action. The abuse, insults and vilification campaign mounted against him by the same class of people that his social reforms were meant for were increasing in intensity.[18] The financial angle involved in the scheme for rehabilitation of families, where widow remarriages took place, became the high points of non-serious jesting and joking even in literature. Towards the end, Vidyasagar arrived at the painful realization that quite a few seemingly willing bridegrooms agreed to marry widows with the sole intention of earning easy money. Bankim in his *Krishnakanter Will* echoed the same sentiment. In this novel Haralal asked Brahmananda if he was willing to earn some money. Brahmananda jokingly answered, 'How, by marrying a widow?'[19]

> We find in *Bishabriksha* (1873) Bankim scoffing at a character who had become a bit of a village oracle. He had read *The Citizen of the World* as well as *The Spectator*, and it was rumoured that he had got through the first three books of geometry. He used to go round telling people, 'Give up worshipping brick and rubble, *get your old aunts married again*, teach women to read and write. Let them out of their cages.' A speciality of his liberal attitude towards women was that there was none in his own

household. Even as late as the 1930s, a popular novelist Sarat Chandra Chatterji did not dare show a remarried widow in any of his novels.[20] (emphasis added)

Bankim's view on widow remarriage, his ambivalence comes out absolutely clearly in his essay on *samya* (equality). 'An examination of his argument will show that the right to remarry was given to widows only to be taken away in the name of chastity and morality.'[21]

In Sarat Chatterji's novel the question of widow remarriage, thrown up time and again, tossed around and viewed from diverse angles was eventually dropped into oblivion perhaps because it was conceived as something hardly conducive to public morality. Nonetheless, the perception and problem of widows and the question of their remarriage remained central to his concerns. To assume that fiction here reflected the social reality would perhaps approximate to the truth. On the other hand the agitation against polygamy and the practice of *Kulinism* was gaining momentum and the reformists, starting from Rammohun Roy and Vidyasagar to the latter day Brahmos, took up cudgels against these systems. But as *Kulin* polygamy concerned a small segment of high caste Brahmins, the agitation against it did not polarize the opinion in society. The Age of Consent Bill created a storm and whipped up arguments and counter arguments in favour and against the social acceptance of any such legislation imposed by alien rulers on the people of an entirely different religious and cultural tradition.

Female education, a necessity of the times, assumed all-pervading significance and agitated the minds of the people from all sections of society equally. Rammohun himself was in favour of educating women and thus raising their social status. Ishwarchandra Vidyasagar established a number of schools for girls, not only in Calcutta, but in far-flung villages in remote districts. Vidyasagar ardently propagated the cause of education for women.

Ishwarchandra Vidyasagar was an ardent supporter of female education and devoted much of his time and energy to the management of the Bethune School during the first 20 years of its existence. Encouraged by its success, albeit limited, he wanted to spread female education in rural Bengal. Between November 1857 and May 1858, he established as many as 35 girls' schools in the districts of Hugli, Burdwan, Midnapur and Nadia. But the schools were soon closed when the Bengal Government withdrew financial support.[22]

Female education in this context was a point where orthodox and progressive reformers converged to create an atmosphere where women of the *bhadralok* class could acquire some attributes to make them better wives and mothers. The educational curriculum they advocated for their women aimed at making them receptive wives and responsible mothers.[23] The stress and strain of working under a colonial superstructure and the pressure of coping with the condescending and very often hostile or humiliating attitudes of the alien rulers sent the English educated Bengali *bhadralok* homeward to look for comfort and consolation. And there appeared the crucial question of a 'sense of loss' or 'missed opportunities'. They had read time and again and seen once in a while the image of the loving wife sitting pretty in a well furnished and carefully decorated living room, welcoming her work-weary husband at the end of the day's labour not only with nutritious food tastefully served, but with conversation intelligently and knowledgeably made to enliven his spirit and soul. With this sort of a picture of 'ideal' Victorian womanhood entrenched in his mind, the Bengali *bhadralok* came back home to find the passage to *antahpur* effectively barred, and his young, often illiterate wife perpetually in *purdah*. His evening spent in the *baithakhana* (the outer quarters) became unwittingly an extension of his work hours. So education meant for women was to promote the cause of men. 'It was argued that an educated wife, rather than neglecting duties, would make a much better housewife than her uneducated counterpart.'[24]

Proper education for women was, moreover, necessary to equip women to act as enlightened and emancipated companions of the English educated Bengali intelligentsia.[25]

His intelligent understanding always prompted him to believe that women had equal claim to education and emancipation. In the course of his debate with his mother and elder brother, he had always put forward the argument that women were human beings too and needed to be released from the secluded existence of the four walls of their home. But now, face to face with this young woman, this guest of their's, he suddenly realised how menfolk were depriving themselves of something immensely valuable by depriving women of their right to education and freedom.[26]

No profounder statement of this sense of loss and its realization could have been made than these utterances of Dwijadas when he was introduced to Vandana in *Bipradas.*

There were no two opinions about the decision that women should be imparted some education. The controversy arose about the content and curriculum to be followed in giving shape to female education. The ultimate objective of education of women, most of the male educators felt, was to develop and encourage the quintessential femininity in women and anything beyond that was perceived as portentious and a threat to the basic fabric of family and society,

We are not against female education. Women should, of course, receive some education and thus free themselves from the clutches of superstition; moreover we expect that education will give them such refinement of character as well as will make them acceptable, as well as respectable to the educated men of Bengal. However, we are against the kind of education now being given to women. . . . The books the women are asked to read are either translation from English or are English-influenced. Consequently, our women become de-nationalised. We believe women should read those books that will help them to become *better wives and better mothers.* This is an age of luxury. Most of the women are luxurious and indifferent to housekeeping and bringing up of their children.[27] (emphasis added)

There had been a plethora of articles and essays, like this one, in journals, including journals meant for women only, advising them on what they should do with their new found opportunities and how they should respond to the expectations expressed by their male counterparts and how to keep themselves within the limits prescribed by the system. The concept of 'denationalization' of women was an interesting conflation of several categories, but at the core of it was the feeling of a threat to male authority; it exposed the ambivalence inherent in the propagation of the idea of female education. This rising—if still subdued—tide of nationalism constructed here in purely cultural terms further reduced to gender, i.e. the female, identity evoking her fickleness and vulnerability—all these mobilized to 'protect' the women from adverse alien influences, that is, to protect the men from the threat of women as educated as themselves. The departure from feminine ideals was not only perceived in the moods and movements of women, but also in their modernized dress codes which consisted of, among other things, shoes and socks. Shoes in particular became a point of fixation with men, for nothing symbolized outward movement beyond the house as effectively as the putting on of shoes in a milieu where shoes are taken off as soon as one enters the walled-in area of the house and worn only when going out again; wearing of shoes had thus come to acquire a gender—male—identity, threatened by a woman wearing them. Ishwar Gupta in his poem, *Durbhiksha*, ridiculed educated modern Bengali women wearing 'boots', driving 'buggies' and smoking cigars and blamed Drinkwater Bethune for robbing them of their womanly virtues.[28] Consider this in the context of Annette Ackroyd Beveridge's comment on no less a person than Keshub Chandra Sen's wife: 'Dressed like a poor wife of some uncultivated Hindoo in red silk wrapper, no shoes and stockings, and a barbaric display of jewels, she sat like a savage who had never heard of dignity and modesty.'[29]

In fiction the 'baneful' effect of Western culture and education on women has figured in the image of a woman in shoes, especially with very high heels. This image has invariably met with disapproval not only of the other characters but of the authors themselves.[30] One could very clearly discern here the inherent contradiction underlying the scheme of women's education and emancipation desired by men. 'They have gained only what men have been willing to grant, they have taken nothing, they have only received.'[31]

This sense of insecurity of men and the fragility of the boundaries erected by them around 'their' women permeated all their arrogant assertions of dominance, subjugation, 'occupation' of women. It is some of this fragility, mediated in literary representation that we have tried to capture in the pages that follow.

NOTES AND REFERENCES

1. Simona Sharoni, 'Every Woman is an Occupied Territory: The Politics of Militarism and Sexism and the Israeli-Palestinian Conflict', *Journal of Gender Studies*, vol. 1, 4 Nov. 1992, pp. 447-62.
2. Michelle Perrot, 'Women, Power and History', in Perrot, ed., *Writing Women's History*, tr. Felicia Pheasant, Oxford: Basil Blackwell, 1992, p. 161.
3. M.Z. Rosaldo and L. Lamphere, *Woman, Culture and Society*, Stanford: Stanford University Press, 1974, p. 9.
4. Natalie Z. Davis, 'Boundaries and the Sense of Self in 16th Century France', in Thomas C. Heller et al., *Reconstructing Individualism: Autonomy, Individuality, and the Self in Western Thought*, Stanford: Stanford University Press, 1986.
5. S.N. Mukherjee, 'Raja Rammohun Roy and the Status of Women in Bengal in the 19th century', in M. Allen and S.N. Mukherjee, eds., *Women in India and Nepal*, Canberra: ANU, 1982, p. 155.
6. For a historical perspective on this problem, see Sumit Sarkar, 'The Women's Question in 19th century Bengal', in Kumkum Sangari and Sudesh Vaid, eds., *Women and Culture*, Bombay: SNDT University, 1985, pp. 157-8.
7. For a detailed list of these periodicals with the articles published in them, see Ghulam Murshid, *Reluctant Debutante: Response of Bengali Women to Modernizaton, 1849-1905*, Rajshahi: Sahitya Samsad, Rajshahi University, 1983, pp. 232-40 and 264-70.
8. See, for example, Humayun Kabir, *Sarat Chandra Chatterjee and the Bengali Novel*. Also see G.V. Raj, *Tagore, the Novelist* and M. Sarada, *Rabindranath Tagore: A Study of Women Characters in his Novels*.
9. For facets of role playing, see Erving Goffman, *The Presentation of Self in Everyday Life*, New York: Doubleday Anchor Books, 1959.
10. Lisa Carol Stamm and D. Ryff, eds., *Social Power and Influence of Women*, AAAS Selected Symposia Series, 1984, p. 3.
11. M.Z. Rosaldo, 'Woman, Culture and Society: A Theoretical Overview', in M.Z. Rosaldo and L. Lamphere, *Woman, Culture and Society*, p. 21.
12. Stamm and Ryff, eds., *Social Power*, p. 4.
13. Michelle Perrot, 'Women, Power and History', in Perrot, ed., *Writing Women's History*, p. 160.
14. K. Nag and D. Burman, eds., *Selected Works of Raja Rammohun Roy*, New Delhi: Govt. of India Publications, 1977, p. 156.
15. Ibid., p. 163.
16. Kumari Jayawardena, *Feminism and Nationalism in the Third World*, New Delhi: Kali for Women, 1986, p. 81.
17. A. Sen, *Vidyasagar and His Elusive Milestones*, Calcutta: Ridhi-India, 1977, p. 60.

18. Ibid., pp. 59-60.
19. Bankimchandra Chatterjee, *Krishnakanter Will*, in *Bankim Rachnavali* (A Collection of Bankimchandra Chatterjee's Novels) vol. I, ed. Yogesh Chandra Bagal, Calcutta: Sahitya Samsad, 1990, p. 428.
20. Meenakshi Mukherjee, *Realism and Reality: The Novel and Society in India*, New Delhi: OUP, 1985, p. 24.
21. A. Poddar, *Renaissance in Bengal: Search for Identity*, Simla: IIAS, 1977, p. 76.
22. G. Murshid, *Reluctant Debutante*, p. 35.
23. See ibid., pp. 56-8. See also M. Borthwick, *The Changing Role of Women in Bengal, 1849-1905*, Princeton: Princeton University Press, 1984.
24. M. Borthwick, p. 64.
25. As Sumit Sarkar has rightly pointed out 'Efforts at education and a *limited* and *controlled* emancipation of wives thus became a personal necessity for survival in the hostile social world'. Sumit Sarkar, *A Critique of Colonial India*, Calcutta: Papyrus, 1985, p. 73.
26. Sarat Chatterjee, *Bipradas*, in *Sarat Rachnavali*, vol. I, Calcutta: Tuli Kalam, 1989, p. 380.
27. '*Streeshiksha O Streeswadhinata*', *Tattvabodhini Patrika*, Nov.-Dec. 1878, pp. 154-6, as quoted in G. Murshid, *Reluctant Debutante*, p. 47.
28. I. Gupta (1812-59), *Durbhiksha*, in S. Gangopadhyaya, ed., *Byanga Kabita O Gane Swadeshikta*, Calcutta, 1977. For a more detailed discussion of the literature of parody and satire in the first half of the nineteenth century, see Partha Chatterjee, *The Nation and its Fragments: Colonial and Postcolonial History*, Delhi: OUP, 1995, pp. 121-4.
29. A. Ackroyd Beveridge, 'Diary and Notebook in India', MSS. Eur., C 176/104, IOLR, London.
30. Sarat Chatterjee, *Nabobidhan*, pp. 793-4; *Bipradas*, pp. 433-5; Tagore, *Shesher Kabita*, p. 777. *Rabindra Rachanavali*, vol. IX, Calcutta: West Bengal Govt. Publication, 1962.
31. Simone de Beauvoir, *The Second Sex*, tr. H.M. Parshley, London: Picador, 1988, p. 19.

CHAPTER 2

Interpersonal Relationships

Interpersonal relationship in its innate diversity encompasses a wide range of both normative human action as well as the individual spaces that often subverted the norms. Keeping in mind the given structure of patriarchal society and the family, we would try to explore the nuances and complexities of interpersonal relationships within the family; we might at times cross its boundaries. The Bengali middle class *bhadralok* society assigned clearly defined roles to different individuals and as long as they adhered to their prescribed roles, the surface placidity, the normalcy could easily be maintained. But there were the 'deviants' and the 'deviations' (termed so by the orthodox society, particularly when they erupted on the women's behaviour) created a parallel stream of action along with the staid, conventional behaviour patterns of the 'normal' human beings.

Interpersonal relationship set on its wide spectrum covers a whole lot of interplay of human behaviour. Some of these are firmly entrenched in socially accepted mainstream behavioural pattern and there lies their legitimacy. People subscribing to the pattern are supposed to be the 'role models' and the female 'role models' generally are 'ideal' mothers, wives—*patibratas* and satis or 'chaste' women—the stereotypes. Although these characters move in predictable contours and predecided confines, we cannot ignore the sheer volume of these characters as they are the ones who constitute the backbone of society. The deviations might be the arteries enriching the complex structure and network of interpersonal relationship. In our present discourse the most vital point to ponder should be the relationship between man and woman—in their diverse moments, with all the pains and pleasures, joys and agonies, stresses and strains entailed in it. But before getting down to it we would like to explore parent-child relationship, particularly parent-female child relationship and the concept of 'ideal' motherhood. Motherhood in our present context conceptualizes the image of the mother not always in the biological sense; it is, on the other hand, visualized as all encompassing universal motherhood—a mother figure to one and all.

> Another key cultural construction of the Hindu kinship system, *mata*, is by no means a simple representation of *dhatra dharma*. Its popular as well as textual usages are so diverse and so figurative that it would be hazardous to try to point out its single most specific denominator. God, for example, quickly becomes a father and a mother at the same time, as in the verse, *twameva matasca pita twameva*. However, returning to common social usages, *mata* is usually a potential or actual mother. . . . The usage is justified by seeing these women as potential or metaphysical mother, they may be seen as mother or mother-like, and in turn these women may be motherly without actually being mothers.[1]

In Bengali society, 'mother' is a cult figure with wide connotations. From the child of six to the old woman of sixty, each one is addressed as *maa* or 'mother' and as a result, any woman could act the role of a mother without restricting herself within the strict boundaries of biological relationships. 'The texture of social communication in Bengal is permeated by the address of mother. This perhaps is the only part of India where the address is used not only by the offsprings and spouses and by servants to the mistress, but to the unknown women in the street and young girls.'[2] The concept of mother is, on the one hand, detached from the person of the mother and thus transformed into an abstraction; on the other, the abstraction is totalizing in its universality that every female irrespective of age or relationship is envisioned as the mother. The concept both limits the woman and invests in her immense power that the mother figure commands in religion, myth and culture. 'Throughout India, the concept of motherhood is revered. The words *mata* and *maa* (mother) connote warmth, protection, life giving power.'[3]

In Bengali fiction, during the period of our analysis, one encounters a number of women who symbolize the eternal mother figure—of mythical *Annapurna* to the people around them. As Leela Dube has observed, 'The ideal of *Annapurna*, the unfailing supplier of food, is accepted across different regions of India'.[4] In the present context, these *Annapurnas* are not only looking after the physical needs of their protégés, they are there to extend their emotional and psychological support, sometimes even at the cost of their biological offsprings' interest. Bishweshwari, in *Palli Samaj* is a remarkable character of this genre. Here in the village society (*palli samaj*) with its narrow, self-centred parochialism, clashes of petty self-interest, exploitation and oppression of the less fortunate members of the society, the dominance of mindless, meaningless religious bigotry and observance of rituals, one stumbles upon a striking individual like Bishweshwari. Here is a woman whose native intelligence, tolerant wisdom and unbiased approach to the village ills mark her out as a cut above the rest of the characters in the novel. And precisely these attributes in her character enable her to take a rational view of unfortunate Rama's dilemma over not being able to hide her real feelings for Ramesh. Bishweshwari, in spite of her deeply felt sympathy and compassion for Rama's agony, cannot visualize any future in her relationship with Ramesh and cannot go beyond the narrow confines of orthodox society's canonical rules meant for the upper caste widows. The only solution she could find for her was in complete renunciation. With genuine love and affection for Rama she said,

> Let's go dear, far away from here to some place where whenever we raise our eyes, there would be neither Beni nor Ramesh but the high pinnacles of the gods' abode and nothing else. I do understand how you feel Rama, but as you are nearing your end, you cannot possibly go there to the other world with this poison of passion hidden in your heart. You and I belong to the highest caste and after our death should reach there in a way befitting the daughters of that caste—the Brahmins.[5]

The tension between an idyllic world—always in the distance, far away—and the existential internalized norms of hierarchy are captured in Bishweshwari's vision and helplessness. And Bishweshwari is truly helpless here, all her sympathy for Rama, all her understanding of her inner conflicts could not envision Rama's attraction for Ramesh as something which can do any good to either of them. It remains the 'poison of passion' as perceived by her and so would it be viewed by the conventional society. Another remarkable character—a quintessential mother is Anandamayee in Tagore's *Gora.* Motherhood assumes an exceptional singularity because of that fine streak of individuality in her character. She was more than a mother to Gora (who was not her real son, which he discovered later) but she was no less a mother to Benoy either, or to Lalita for that matter. She decided to be present at Benoy's wedding against the express wishes of her son Gora who, passing through an orthodox *Hindutva* phase, was opposed to this marriage as Lalita was from a Brahmo family and orthodox Hindu society could not have accepted this union as something desirable. Anandamayee with her quiet strength of conviction could thwart the petty, humdrum dictates of the powers that be, and abided by the prompting of her own belief that whatever Benoy and Lalita were about to do had the moral and ethical, if not social sanction. Not only did she attend the wedding but accepted Lalita as the daughter she had long been waiting for and did so with such dignity that it put Lalita's father's agitated and disturbed mind to rest.

From these images of sublime motherhood, we come down to Rajlakshmi in *Chokher Bali* an average commonplace mother whose whole world revolved around her only son Mahendra with all his whims, eccentricities and frivolities. Behari, Mahendra's close friend, was almost a son to her. But the fact remained, he was her son by proxy, not her real son and when there was a possibility of a clash of interest, Rajlakshmi did not hesitate for a moment to side with her own son, however unreasonable the stand assumed by him. All her heartburn, all her clashes and conflicts with other members of the family, Annapurna, Asha, Binodini and even Behari were caused by her blind, all absorbing love and affection for her only son and her desire to keep her supreme control over him intact. A mother of her sort was perhaps accepted as a role model in the middle class society in our country and could easily be put in the category of stereotypical Bengali mother.

Coming back to the concept of assumed or surrogate motherhood, we find it quite a common occurrence reinforcing the idea of the presence of mother psyche in all women irrespective of their age or status in the family or in society. Parbati in *Debdas*, hardly out of her teens, was a most unlikely person to assume the role of a mother to her grown up step children, but she did exactly that, and with perfect ease.[6] How far this role assumption was out of her sense of duty to her husband, or of what was expected of her and how far was it genuine motherly feeling would always remain an open question. The contemporary social perception of a 'fallen woman' like Rajlakshmi in *Shrikanta* would not obviously have allowed her even to dream of her own children 'Rajlakshmi in *Shrikanta* (similarly) remained unfulfilled because of the tension between her love and her beliefs'.[7] 'Woman's ultimate fulfilment lies in her attaining motherhood and this can be said without an iota of doubt.'[8] Motherhood eluded Rajlakshmi, in spite of her long relationship with Shrikanta, a relationship which did not always remain outside the closed bedroom door.[9] It apparently went against her ingrained 'belief' as part of her socialization to express even a desire to have a normal conjugal life with Shrikanta and bear his children. All her life she had to pretend that she was happy enough to have her stepchildren around her and treat them as her own.[10]

In a society where women have always occupied a position of subordination and subjugation, where they have always been held responsible for any misfortune befalling the family be it the irresponsible behaviour of a wayward husband or the impoverishment of the father, of a not so well endowed unmarried daughter, it's easy to imagine the situation a female child would be placed in. And when it comes to the mother-daughter relationship we find it marked by an acute sense of guilt, self-reproach and helplessness on both sides. Guilt, because of producing a daughter who is going to be a life-long liability and helplessness and frustration, because in spite of all her love and affection for her unfortunate daughter, unfortunate only because she is a girl, the mother finds it beyond her power, sometimes her express will, to redress the wrong done to her. (Of course with the spread of female education and liberal outlook in the *bhadralok* society we find a perceptible change in the attitude towards the girl child. But this change is reflected in the father-daughter relationship; the mother's preoccupation primarily remains the marriage of the daughter, that too at an appropriate age, thus reinforcing the notion of the daughter as a liability.)

In Bankim's *Debichoudhurani*, both Prafulla and her mother were the victims of an unequal and hostile society. Immediately after her marriage Prafulla was shunted off to her poor widowed mother, with the accusation that her mother had a questionable past. Prafulla, exasperated by utter penury raised the question as to why should she suffer like this when her in-laws were living in plenty. Her mother, instead of blaming others, characteristically took all the blame on herself: 'Your crime is you were born to this unlucky mother and then there is your destiny.'[11] In Sarat's *Arakshania* we find a peculiar emotional clash between the mother's feeling of affection and her sense of social obligation. In a society where girls are supposed to be given away in marriage before they attain puberty,[12] the title of this novelette carries a significant import. If not married at a proper age, a girl would be beyond protection. Protection provided by men against other men—pointing to the dual vulnerability of women, as persons and as social beings. Reinforcing this vulnerability is the social stigma attached to women whose sexual chastity is violated by men, stigma that finds expression in the religious idiom of sin, which would invoke eternal punishment for women. The relation between Gyanada and Durgamani, daughter and mother is that of a very deep and silent understanding—each could see the agony the other was going through. Durgamani, predictably enough, blamed herself for bringing a daughter into this world, 'I don't know what sin did I commit in my previous birth that I had to give birth to a daughter'.[13] This is an utterance not necessarily out of any real sense of hostility towards the daughter but simply the outcome of a helpless mother's anguish and frustration. And yet the idiom is that of sin, of eternal punishment, of accursed motherhood if it brings forth a daughter rather than a son.

The presence of a son is absolutely necessary for proper performance of many sacraments, especially those carried out upon the death of his parents and imperative to the well being of their souls. In addition to her ritual significance, a daughter normally is an unmitigated expense, someone who will never contribute to the family income and who, upon marriage, will take away a considerable part of her family's fortune as her dowry. In the case of a poor family, the parents may even have to go deep in debt in order to provide for a daughter's marriage.[14]

But then, affection does exist in the everlasting situation of frustration and pain. The same mother seeing the daughter cowering under the threat of a forced marriage with a widower much older in age, comforted her: 'As long as I am alive, child, nobody can touch you.'[15] But the very next moment the futility of her assurance became clear to her. Sooner or later, she knew she would have to accept the dictates of her milieu, succumb to the societal pressure to give away her daughter, however unworthy the groom. In the end she allowed herself to be pressurized to accept a proposal of marriage for her daughter with a much married widower.

This feeling of helpless guilt and self-reproach is nowhere so pronounced as in the case of Shubha's mother.[16] The mute Shubha was more her mother's responsibility than her father's. Her mother accepted her daughter's disability as a symbol of her own failings. The mother is always more inclined to consider her daughter as a part of her own being. Any disability that appears in the daughter becomes particularly a matter of shame for the mother.[17] The irony of the situation becomes all the more heartbreaking as Shubha's mother played an active role in arranging her daughter's marriage keeping the bridegroom's party in the dark about her disability and thereby shoving her helpless and vulnerable daughter into the jaws of unfamiliar, unfriendly and certain to be hostile destiny.

Not that this sort of helplessness in the face of the combined force of society, culture, tradition and one's beliefs and *samskaras* is indiscernible in father-daughter relationship too. The only difference is that at any crucial moment the society permits the father to take a particular decision to safeguard the interest of the daughter as in the case of Nirupama's father, Ramsundar.[18] Ramsundar being at the end of his tether decided to sell off his ancestral dwelling unit to make good his promise of dowry which he was unable to give at the time of her marriage.[19] The mothers without any economic independence, any effective authority in the household matters and in most of the cases with practically non-existent property rights could never have thought of even suggesting such a step.[20]

Kedarnath in *Gribadaba*[21] is a father bound by conventionality and his expectations and aspirations regarding his daughter did not go much beyond the traditional ambience of the society they lived in. Quite naturally, his relationship with his daughter was more or less confined within the predictable framework of socially approved behavioural patterns. As a conventional father of a motherless daughter, the foremost concern in his life was to see his daughter happily married. And to his mind, a happy marriage did not have any other meaning than to see his daughter in the midst of prosperity. 'His notion of marital expectation was that the women would always prefer a husband who could provide them with big houses, good carriages and plenty of clothes and ornaments. The intricacy of conjugal relationship, the concept of love in marriage were things beyond his comprehension.'[22] And consequently his obvious preference was for Suresh as Achala's husband. But once Achala made her choice and married Mahim, for her father it was the final, irrevocable decision. When Achala came back from Mahim's village, and came back alone with Suresh, his sense of social morality and propriety, of ethics, indeed of social order was seriously jolted and he squarely blamed both Suresh and Achala for this unseemly conduct.

> Mahim was not exactly the apple of his eye, but that his own daughter would do something so shameful as to leave her husband's house and be completely oblivious of the duties and responsibilities of a woman, was something beyond his wildest dreams. Achala had committed a sin and Suresh was instrumental in helping her do it and his attitude towards Suresh changed completely.[23]

His Brahmo background notwithstanding, even the suggestion of his daughter violating the norm of a *patibrata* was something absolutely unimaginable for him. Yet, in the tension between socially created norms of behaviour and the basic human instinct of affection for the offspring, humanity overrides social norms and the father would defy society in extending forgiveness to his errant daughter. This, not quite in the face of society but at a distance from it. In spite of all her deviant acts, he would have her back and take care of her even at the cost of leaving society and living in wilderness, the father and the daughter all by themselves.[24]

In Tagore's short story 'Haimanti' the relation between Haimanti and her father[25] was based on a more constructive and meaningful exchange of views of two equal minds. The same strain of uprightness and truthfulness, the same streak of wit and humour could be found both in the father and the daughter. The attitudinal change towards daughters that was taking place in this particular social milieu is quite clearly discernible here. The daughters were no longer treated as sheer burdens on their parents; they could also provide rare companionship. Haimanti and her father's last meeting[26] underlines the exchange of two rational minds though the undercurrent of deep tragedy and sense of anguish was easily visible. In 'Haimanti' the young husband appears to be absolutely helpless, in spite of his deep love and affection for his wife and complete understanding of her feelings. This helplessness was not exactly born out of his inability to rescue his wife from under the severe restrictions and disciplining of his unsympathetic parents. It was more out of a sense of social norm and social behaviour expected of him. He sacrificed his true feelings for the sake of social priorities and sense of propriety. This is also a part of one's ingrained socialization. That a man should be prepared to sacrifice his true love to please his parents or others for that matter, is reminiscent of the Ramchandra syndrome. His inability or the absence of his determination and a strong will to come out of this stranglehold is agonizingly explicit in his ironical and self-depreciatory comments, 'That day when the people of Ayodhya clamoured for Sita's banishment, I was present there. When people sang in praise for this magnificent sacrifice on the part of Rama, I joined them. Is it not only the other day I wrote an article glorifying the virtues of this sacrifice?'[27] The conduct of Haimanti's husband is at least understandable, but all the 'rationality' of the person to person relationship between Haimanti and her father lost its lustre in a moment of crisis pointing to the fragility of a rational, equal relationship in a situation of socially conditioned dependence, on both her husband and, in this crisis, her father; the father's on the expectation of his daughter's marital bliss, deriving from his aloofness in case she survived.[28] On the other hand in the case of 'Aparichita'[29] the father could afford to be much more forthright in showing his integrity and iron will and could send the bridegroom's party back along with the groom before the marriage could be solemnized. Here the risk involved was much less in magnitude as the daughter was not already married. In this case the bridegroom's uncle's contention that the father would try to cheat on them, and could give his daughter less amount of gold than promised was preposterous. It was a direct affront to his sense of self-respect, honesty and integrity and that is why he could deal with it so swiftly and decisively. In 'Haimanti', the daughter's well-being was uppermost in her father's mind, whereas in 'Aparichita', the father had to think of his injured sense of self-respect and personal prestige. 'I can't think of giving my daughter away to the people who can accuse the father of cheating his daughter.'[30] Kalyani in 'Aparichita', after this matrimonial debacle decided to remain unmarried and devote her time and life to the service of her 'motherland'. Her decision obviously is an improvement on the lot of 'Arakshania' and her likes. This decision once again reflects on 'social sanction' and the attitudes of the elite class of the time.[31] Another important point to ponder would be the fact that both Kalyani and Haimanti were reared and nurtured away from the stifling and suffocating ambience of orthodox Hindu rural society as Gyanada, in 'Arakshania', had to see herself confined to. Both Kalyani and Haimanti were parts of *probasi* Bengali families and thereby could expect and experience some sort of basic changes in attitudes towards women and their activities.

The wide sweep of time covered here starting from Bankim's Prafulla to Tagore's Kalyani—the broad spectrum of men and women with vastly diverse social, economic, cultural and educational backgrounds—help construct an image of a period in transition. The perception of society regarding the role and status of women was undergoing noticeable mutations. One can easily perceive the change in the conception of parents on how to bring up their daughters and devise ways and means to make them aware of their individuality. This we find in 'Aparichita', to some extent in 'Haimanti' and in *Jogajog*[32] in the case of Kumudini though she was brought up under the tutelage of her elder brother Bipradas. But surprisingly, in spite of the 'liberating' process sweeping through the *bhadralok* society of the said period, the predominant worry in the mind of the parents, irrespective of their status in society, remained the marriage of the daughter and marriage at appropriate time, to be precise. This dichotomy, this ambivalence of the situation, indicates the limits of the liberating processes though it is not necessary to question the intentions of the men in seeking to equip their daughters to deal with life in a more adequate and competent manner.

The most vital component of all relationships, the man-woman relation, including the relationship between husband and wife necessarily calls for a more detailed exploration. And here, as a matter of course, one has to deal with the concept of *patibrata* as conceived in the patriarchal set up prevalent in family life. While venturing into the realm of man-woman/husband-wife relationship, we must keep in mind that the predominant concern in a traditional male-dominated society was the chastity or *satitva* or *patibratya* of a wife. Ethel Spector Parson points out:

> It has long been recognised that certain conventions—the double standard, the cult of virginity, and the requirement that female sexuality find expression solely within monogamous heterosexual marriages—control and inhibit female sexuality. Whatever their origins might be, these conventions are major support for male dominance and patriarchy.[33]

This is the only criterion which will determine the virtue of the wife and any deviation would pose a threat to male authority and balance of power so assiduously maintained. What is more, this male perception is internalized by women without much apparent protest or questioning. As long as the wife is *patibrata*, men could easily assume the role of the protector and provider. Cutting across the various strata of society, the concept of *patibrata* wife held a strong sway over the minds of the individuals. The 'venerated' name of Manu still had a strong hold over the male psyche. When we turn to fiction, we find innumerable instances within the male paradigm of *patibrata* wife and it is no wonder that women, as a result of sustained socialization, accept this role model as an ideal to emulate. The social construction of the role of an ideal woman, in an uncomplicated and benign situation, is nowhere so eminently evident as in the case of Bimala's mother in *Ghare Baire*.[34] It is a brief narration; in a nutshell, it enumerates what a *patibrata*, a sati or a chaste woman should be, and how she should relate to her husband. This image remained a reference point for Bimala and the legitimacy assumed by it becomes all the more significant when we find Bimala absolutely distraught with grief at the thought of herself deviating from the path shown by her mother—the path to be followed by a dutiful chaste wife.[35] She reminisced:

> In my childhood I have seen how the complete devotion (wife's devotion to her husband) lends an aura of rare charm and beauty to everything around it. I have seen with what loving care my mother would arrange fruit pieces on my father's plate, how she would keep aside the beautifully made 'pan' leaves wrapped in essence soaked cloth specially for him. At his meal time how she would sit by his side gently wafting the hand fan to keep away flies—the whole image interlaced with her love, affection and sense of selfless devotion made a tremendous impact on my mind even as a child.[36]

For Bimala's mother the transition from the seclusion and the loving protection of parental home to those of her husband's family must have been a smooth one; so had been the transformation from a precious daughter to a beloved wife. In Annadadidi in *Shrikanta* we come across the instance of a woman clinging on to the concept of *patibratya* against all odds and in absolutely hostile surroundings. Her *patibratya* is manifested in the fact that she never talked ill of a husband who was nothing less than a hardened criminal and served him devotedly until the very end. In doing so she was merely following Manu's injunction: 'A virtuous wife should constantly serve her husband like a god, even if he behaves badly, freely indulges his lust, and is devoid of any good qualities.'[37]

Annada's husband disappeared from her father's house after committing the murder of Annada's widowed elder sister. In her last letter to Shrikanta, she wrote, 'What prompted him to do such a reprehensible act, you are too young to comprehend; but you will understand the reason when you grow up.'[38]

Annada had to put up with this terrible shame. But when after seven long years this husband of her's appeared in her life as a Muslim snake charmer, she left home with him. The perception of the people around her was that she had left home with a stranger and she had to carry this burden of shame all her life. She herself considered it (her husband's act and what she consequently did) a 'terrible shame', 'the humiliation she could never forget'. Then why did she in the first place leave her sheltered existence behind for something entirely unknown? She very clearly did not have any illusion about her husband. When he claimed that he did the daring act of appearing in front of her father's house for her sake only, she could dismiss it as a shameless lie. 'Of course, that was a lie. But all the same, at the dead of the night, by the back door of the house, I left home only for my husband.'[39]

Faced with a forced celibacy, which she did not appear to have cherished, she would rather surrender to what was perhaps her repressed, though live sexuality, which could be satiated only if she 'eloped' with her husband, however socially stigmatized he might be. The tension deriving from a decision that can only bring perpetual shame is teleologically subdued in her apparent conformity to the social ideal laid by Manu. Nevertheless a certain boldness on her part to court endless blasphemy sets her apart from total submission.

Suryamukhi stood up for herself in a slightly different kind of way, though still proclaiming adherence to Manu's ideals. For her,

> the only source of all my happiness in this world is my husband. If I ever bother about anything in my life it is about my husband. The only thing I value most in this world is once again my husband.[40]

> Above all, in the ideals of the traditional culture, the 'good' woman is a *pativrata*, subordinating her life to the husband's welfare and needs. . . .[41]

Suryamukhi is a woman who received basic education under

an English governess and was fairly enlightened in her outlook; her protestation of total self-effacement vis-à-vis her husband, however, does not disguise her strong personality as she determinedly took the ultimate step of leaving home and to face the unknown, after her husband brought in his second wife, Kundanandani.

Embedded in the concept of *patibratya* was the notion of sexual fidelity, the single-minded devotion to one man; consequently to be considered a good woman was to remain 'faithful to one man not only through this life but in all subsequent ones'.[42] Once again this concept is a male construction, for it was not reciprocated by men; it was, however, internalized by women and it could quite effectively seal out the possibility of any deviation—physical deviation at least. Yet some sort of an infidelity, which might appear in some deep recess of the mind and itself violative of *patibratya*, did surface and we shall discuss it later. For Surobala,[43] being the object of her husband's love and care, to think of this relationship extending from this life to the next was not a difficult proposition and with supreme confidence she could utter, 'wherever were I, wherever were I born you had to go there to accept me as your wife'.[44]

But for Mrinal in *Gribadaba* it was a conscious decision having been reinforced by the Hindu concept of *punarjanma* (rebirth) and of undying devotion of the wife to her lord and master. As we are told in the narrative:

> This is not a relationship of this life alone—it goes on from this life to the next and so on. I had been given in marriage to one whose *dasi* (slave) I am. Marriages are made in heaven and entirely independent of human wishes and desires.[45]

To remain *patibrata*, to be absolutely devoted to one's husband, to subordinate all one's wishes to the husband's pleasure was and still is considered the highest attribute of a woman's character. But sometimes there arose situations when women were forced to choose between their wifely obligations and obligation to what they considered to be even more sublime than being *patibrata* at any cost. It is most fascinating to come across women, in no way out of the ordinary and quite conventional to start with, going against ingrained socialization which teaches them to treat their husbands as lords and masters and to be ever submissive to their wishes.

In Bengali fiction of this period we often find characters going beyond and defying any stereotyped mould. Shashi in Tagore's 'Didi'[46] is a *patibrata* as long as her *patibratya* did not clash with her basic sense of good and bad, the basic ethics and morality that—she felt should guide all human actions, and these transcend the handed down order of things. Shashi thus appropriated morality and decentred it from the male dominated social order. Shashi, as we have already observed, was a typical *patibrata* to start with.

> How she had defied and quarrelled with her husband over small little things; now she resolved, with remorse in her heart, not only not to show any impatience, but to carry out all his wishes, to put up with all his good, bad or indifferent treatment with love and with good humour and to treat her husband as her god.[47]

The same Shashi left the *antahpur* and pleaded with the British magistrate and complained against her husband who was out to deprive her helpless young orphan brother of his rightful inheritance. She was prepared to go to any extent to protect the interest of her brother in the hostile world around them. To her this was a cause with much more ethical value and her sense of responsibility was strong enough to defy her husband's instructions and injunctions and social strictures too.[48] For this cause she was prepared to sacrifice her own life and life's happiness which she ultimately did. There is also a role reversal here: a woman standing up for the defence of a male and even dying in defence of a just cause—again normatively a male preserve. Then, Shashi dies defending her natal family against the unjust marital family, whereas normatively her loyalty, once married, should have been entirely to her husband's family. The fact that the male being defended by her was a young child, rather than a grown up, perhaps suggests that the phenomenon of a woman's determination to rise to the defence of men was itself in its infancy.

Kusum's *patibratya* in 'Drishtidan'[49] is of a different nature altogether. She is not a typical *patibrata* of *Manusmriti*. Soon after she lost her eyesight, thanks to her doctor husband's inexperienced handling of the whole thing, she did insist that her husband should marry again. She perhaps wanted to spare her husband the agony of being saddled with a blind wife for the rest of his life. Her husband at that juncture took a severe vow *'ami jeno bramha hatya, pitr hatyar pataki hoi'* (If ever I marry again, I would be burdened with the sin of murdering my father and a Brahmin as well.)[50]

But after a few years' gap Kusum, to her utter dismay, discovered that her husband was preparing for his second marriage. She was absolutely disconsolate at the thought of her husband forgetting the vow he had taken in the name of their family deity. She would rather accept her widowhood than to see her husband breaking his vow. All her protestations and entreaties were in vain. Her husband left to bring home the new bride.

> I closed the doors of my *puja* room and started offering prayers. The whole day I stayed inside. In the evening, there came a terrible storm which shook even the foundation of the building. I did not ever say, 'O God, my husband is still on the disturbed river in his boat, save his life'. I only said, 'Whatever may happen to me, let it be, but you must stop my husband from committing this grave sin'.[51]

Even as the story line and the plot are different here from the preceding one, there is nevertheless a thematic unity: while the man is bound to the mundane and the petty, it is the woman who stands out as the repository of a higher morality and paying a terrible price for it. All too subtly, all the received wisdom about male superiority and grandeur and the quotidian feminine existence are being pushed to the background and the quiet aura of feminine strength has been forgrounded.

If we turn our attention from the concept of *patibrata* woman as the *dasi* of her husband to the image of the wife as *grhini saciva sakhi meetho priyoshishya lolitey kalabidhou* we will notice some perceptible change in the conjugal relationship. Enlightened and educated Bengali *bhadralok* of this period visualized as well as propagated the image of ideal wifehood as not only consisting of a series of uncomplaining services rendered to her 'lord and master', but in her ability to share and contribute to the trials and tribulations as well as the moments of happiness and achievements of her husband. But in spite of the apparent changes in conjugal relationships, there was 'no major change in conjugal roles'.[52] Bengali men always wanted their women to be perfect home makers. Any question of equal rights, independent thinking or attempt to seek out one's identity in the case of a woman was frowned upon. Women should be sweet, innocent and trusting, having full faith in the husband's decision and wisdom.[53] Too many questions asked, too inquisitive and independent a mind[54] would cause a potential threat to the carefully maintained balance of power in the society and spell ultimate doom for all, including the woman concerned.[55] Even keen intelligence or anything resembling an intellectual quest was looked upon as something unbecoming of a woman[56] and therefore a deviation.

But, of course, one aspect of the emerging Bengali *bhadralok* consciousness of this period was undeniably the woman's question, the question of alleviating the status of women in society. Bengali men often started the process from within the confines of the *antahpur* by imparting education to their wives and daughters. The Tagore family was in the forefront in this respect in educating the daughters and daughters-in-law and turning them in the process into enlightened and accomplished individuals.[57] There were other families too, particularly among the Brahmos who wanted to emulate the Tagores and had accepted them as their role model. Women coming out of the *purdah* and receiving a certain amount of education albeit within a restricted curriculum were more or less the order of the day, at least in the educated society of the Bengali elites.

> Formal education became not only acceptable but, in fact, a requirement for the new *bhadromohila* (respectable woman) when it was demonstrated that it was possible for a woman to acquire the cultural requirements afforded by modern education without jeopardizing her place at home, that is, without becoming a *memsahib*.[58]

And this paradigm shift in its place led to some changes, some improvement in the conjugal relationship.[59] The concept of companionate marriage gradually started taking shape in the mind of the elite Bengali society. One fine example of this is portrayed in Tagore's *Ghare Baire.* Nikhilesh always wanted his wife to relate to him on an equal footing. He never expected his wife to worship him. He on his part did the worshipping, as Bimala enumerates: 'You have loved my body as if it was some rare flower of the paradise, you have considered my mind and my nature as some rare gift of your good fortune.'[60]

In their interpersonal, conjugal relationship Nikhilesh endeavoured to introduce the concept of equality of status,[61] but did he indeed? A closer look at the relationship would point to a somewhat elusive equality. Economically, women continued to depend entirely upon the men's munificence. The question of political rights was not even on the agenda in a sphere of existence that was exclusively the men's preserve. Nonetheless, it was a step forward, a step towards partial and gradual emancipation of women within the family and therefore in society.

The man-woman relationship or, more precisely women's response to the male dominated society where they had to play a subordinate role all the time and their attempt to define their relationship to the opposite sex is a highly interesting proposition to evaluate. In the changing social scenario, this relationship can broadly be categorized at three levels. First, of course, is the one where husband and wife outwardly maintain a comfortably placid conjugal relationship where the husband is kind and considerate and the wife is always grateful for the mercy. We have here in this category the relationship between Surobala and Upendra,[62] which we have referred to earlier. Tagore with his incisive insight into human nature could very easily lay bare the true relationship between a man and a woman. In his 'Patro O Patri',[63] he deftly delineates 'ideal' conjugal relationship, the highest conjugal happiness. Here the husband is most condescendingly protective and possessive towards his wife and the wife is expected to consider herself fortunate to have occupied the status of the wife of a successful man, and should bend backwards as far as possible to accommodate the wishes, trivial or serious, of her esteemed husband. Sanat Kumar, the hero of the story, had a very clear-cut image of the conjugal bliss before him. Had he not watched his parents' relationship all his life?

> I have seen my mother all my life and I know what one should expect from one's wife. I know my father too, he would ridicule all religious rituals and *bratas*, but when it was the time for *Savitri brata* (which wives devoutly observed for the long life and prosperity of their husbands), he would feel considerably pleased. There was no doubt that my mother loved him dearly, but her perpetual state of fear, her apprehension that some of her actions might cause his annoyance or anger were the things he, with all his masculine identity, used to enjoy most.[64]

The same mindset, the same attitude of taking one's wife for granted is visible in 'Poila Number'. Here the husband, supposedly more enlightened and much more liberated, did not for a moment hesitate to assign to his exceptionally intelligent and capable wife the only role of an accommodating spouse serving him and his cronies silently without any protest. That the wife could come out of this stranglehold and decide her own future which she eventually did, was possible only because of her quiet strength of conviction and character. This sort of ambivalent attitude of the Bengali middle class characterized the whole of the nineteenth century. There always seemed to be some confusion, some doubts in the sphere of social reforms about how far the women should be given the freedom to determine their own destiny and assert their identity.

In the second category, we find women like Achala[65] and Bimala,[66] both educated and articulate with a certain amount of exposure to the outside world. Both of them overstepped the boundaries of proper behaviour although under different circumstances and had to pay for their actions. At the end both of them were overwhelmed by their individual sense of guilt and remorse. Between these two characters, Achala had to face a situation much more complex and grievous and it created absolutely insurmountable social and moral upheavals in her life which left her utterly destitute in the end. This situation to some extent was the creation of Achala herself. Achala it seems did not know her own mind. Her love for Mahim and her attraction towards Suresh had affected her actions with equal force and she was torn between these two conflicting emotions.[67] The secret equally lies in the characters of the two protagonists. Mahim with the rare strength and depth of character, his honesty and truthfulness had attracted Achala's respect and love, perhaps in that order. But he was lacking in overt demonstrativeness and articulation about his emotions. Suresh, on the other hand, was basically an impulsive man. His initial infatuation and subsequent genuine attraction towards Achala was absolutely transparent. Achala was for some time utterly confused and perplexed about her own reaction to Suresh's undivided attention. In the meantime, there crept in some doubts in her mind about Mahim and the genuineness of his feelings. This indecisiveness on her part has been attributed to her training and upbringing as a Brahmo woman. The Brahmos, unlike the Hindus, were not completely averse to the idea of a second marriage or leaving one's husband and taking a second one.[68] The unflinching, unwavering devotion of the Hindu woman to the idea of monogamy, sacred in death as much as in life, was not an integral part of Achala's upbringing. Mrinal at one point expressed this idea of the 'true' Hindu woman: 'To us our husband is our *dharma*, as we cannot change it so we cannot change our husbands; he is forever the same, in life as well as in death.'[69]

Achala was in no way a passive tool in the hand of a scheming villain, which Suresh at any rate was not. Achala, in her interaction with Suresh, had always expressed a tolerant and sympathetic understanding, if not conscious approval, of his feelings. Suresh's love for Achala had a romantic aura about it, which Mahim's sedate self-effacing affection entirely lacked. Quite naturally, Achala's mood alternated between her devotion to her husband and her attraction towards the 'other' man in her life. In the process she was forever burdened with a sense of shame for being indulgent to Suresh and consequently appearing unfaithful to her husband. But what is more interesting and what actually gives us an insight into the changing self-perception of a woman is the fact that her sense of shame or guilt could not completely stop her from glorying in the knowledge of Suresh's unbounded love for her[70] or from the defiance she had shown to her husband and the village society in the process.[71] This sort of a phase in the life of an educated, enlightened young woman was not entirely unheard of. Achala would easily have got over it had Suresh not dragged her out of her secure niche and thrown her over into the wide world where, for her sheer physical survival, and to retain the tenuous hold on her hope of acceptability in the immediate society, she had to act as his wife and had to lead a life of deceit and falsehood. No amount of education and modernization could give her enough strength to obliterate the sense of loss and shame when she had to spend a night with Suresh in his bedroom[72] which she did, once again, to keep the image of husband-wife relationship intact in the eyes of her immediate neighbours. This intense conflict between one's personal and one's social identities expressed in terms of sexual relationships returns again and again in the realm of women's thought and behaviour in this period. It emphatically qualifies the 'emancipation' of women from the ambivalence of their relationship to themselves, the men and the patriarchal society that enveloped their social being. Yet, the conflict equally qualified their total subjugation to their 'other'—the men.

In the case of Bimala, the situation is slightly different. Here the husband himself was trying to bring his wife out of the *purdah*, introduce her to the outside world, moulding her personality from a mere wife to an individual.[73] Bimala's husband, Nikhilesh was a twentieth-century man in the true sense of the term, at least according to his wife.[74] At one time, Bimala did not attach much value to her husband's contention that a woman needed to come out of the four walls to realize her own worth as well as her husband's.

> People talk about women as birds in a cage and all that. I don't know about others, but there was so much of space inside the cage for me that the whole world would not have been enough to contain it. At least that's what I used to think then.[75]

Then there appeared the other man in Bimala's life, Sandeep, a friend of Nikhilesh's. Sandeep, from the very beginning, started working on Bimala's sentiments and feelings which eventually was made easier by his professed unwavering devotion to the cause of the country's freedom and selfless sacrifice for it, but which was imbued with mutual sexual attraction, though never overtly expressed. Bimala was completely 'swept off her feet'[76] and prepared to go against her husband's express wishes. Nikhilesh did not subscribe to Sandeep's type of patriotism; he became a helpless spectator when he found his wife drifting away from him more and more, and he was too much of a gentleman to use force or to intervene in this matter. Nikhilesh, with his intellectual insight, could visualize the upheaval in their marital relationship and could see its roots in the mental make up of Bimala, and in shortcomings innate to her, and some to his own, nature. Nikhilesh, by disposition, had always been soft and sensitive; his sense of justice and fairplay and the immense amount of sympathetic understanding of human nature, particularly of women's nature (which he had shown in his compassionate and sensitive dealings with his widowed sisters-in-law, and which had always been perceived by Bimala as a weakness) marked him out as a person diametrically opposite to Sandeep. Sandeep, on the other hand, was aggressive and blatantly assertive and these were the things which made him irresistible to Bimala, who always secretly lamented the lack of this conventional masculinity in her husband's character. It becomes evident in Nikhilesh's statement,

> Somewhere, something in my character has remained beyond Bimala's comprehension. I, on my part, always feel that one uses force out of one's inherent weakness, and weak people can never wait for justice to take its due course. But patience in a man's character does not impress Bimala. She prefers men to be angry, impatient and even unjust and feels overwhelmed by them. She feels her respect for her man should be mingled with a sense of fear.[77]

Later he says, 'it is not a question of lack of understanding, it is rather a question of two basically different natures'.[78]

Bimala was basically an overly pampered individual,[79] who, because of her husband's delicate handling of her emotional as well as physical needs[80] had assumed the role of a very special person with immense power over the opposite sex. Interestingly, Bimala all along in her strong attraction towards Sandeep visualized the picture of impending doom and destruction. Overriding her own ambivalence was the concern with social limits—which, if crossed, would inevitably and inexorably result in personal disaster. She was always mortally afraid of any sign of aggression from Sandeep's side. It was quite clear to her that she could or should never cross the limits which would violate the concept of *satitva*—any deviation from the accepted code of conduct. The undercurrent of sexuality was quite apparent in their relationship and that was the 'danger' she tried to avert as much as she welcomed it. 'It (whatever Sandip told her) sent my heart racing. It was at hand—the danger. How could I stop the onslaught. It was an experience terrifying and full of elation at the same time and how to cope with it was just beyond my power.'[81]

The crux of the situation which lent complexity to it is exactly this factor—this mingling of joy, elation and fear. Bimala was standing at the threshold of something ominous—ominous in the perception of society and her own self. 'It does portend my fall. I'll have to fall face down on to the dust of the road' (*amake je pather dhulor opor mukh thubde podte hobe*)[82]—*pather dhulo* meant to signify one's departure from the norms of respectability and the absence of familial support which ultimately ends in desertion by one's kin. This desertion might not always be physical, but one's existence would be on the razor's edge all the same. This realization, at least in Bimala's case, could not dissuade her from glorying in her power as a woman and her relationship with Sandeep was based on the dual sense of glory and triumph as well as of guilt and shame. Similarly, Achala's desperation was equally apparent when after Suresh's death she enquired from her husband about some destitute women's home and of the possibility of spending the rest of her life there.[83]

In the third category of man-woman relationship we find women like Binodini, a young widow, and Kiranmayee, a neglected wife who was eventually widowed. According to the restrictive social convention, they were supposed to lead a marginal existence but tried to occupy centre stage by the dint of their determination to set right some of the wrongs done to them. Out of the frustrations of a deprived life, a loveless, sexless existence where, at least in the case of Kiranmayee, one had to compromise one's sense of honour or personal choice for the sake of sheer physical survival, with tacit support and encouragement of the mother-in-law.[84] Kiranmayee's character, when she was introduced in the novel, did appear to be an enigma to the people around her. At the initial stage of their acquaintance, Upendra and Satish had very different perceptions of her character. Upendra along with Satish had gone to visit his critically ill friend Haran Babu and came face to face with Kiranmayee. Satish was openly critical of her lack of concern for her husband, her behaviour and the way she had taken care of her personal appearance. He could not find anything in her behaviour to suggest the perturbed mental state of a grieving wife. Upendra, on the other hand, was much more understanding and sympathetic.[85] Satish, on their way back from Haran Babu's house, tried to remind Upendra of the potential danger underlying the familiarity with a very attractive young woman, with her husband on the deathbed. Satish could not reconcile himself to the idea that Kiranmayee had taken extra care to appear attractive in spite of the fact that her husband was on the verge of death. To add to his suspicion about her character, he found her husband not showing much concern about her future while making the final settlement of his house and some money. Satish, predictably, arrived at the conclusion that Kiranmayee was not a real *patibrata*.[86] Obviously the threat Satish foresaw emanating from Kiranmayee was the threat which always agitated the minds of the upholders of morality in society—the threat of the latent sexuality of a woman, without any socially sanctioned outlet open to them. In any case, Kiranmayee's pragmatic attitude—one might even term it a cynical attitude—towards life derived from the assumption that sexuality was central to the relationship between man and woman, irrespective of their ages. This sets her apart from all other women characters of Sarat (except perhaps for Kamal in *Sheshprashna*) and of other contemporary writers as well. In the course of her discussion with Dibakar about what true love was, she stated in a matter of fact way that love was nothing but uncontrollable physical desire—urge for the opposite sex—one might adorn it with some ornamental decorations and pass it on as 'heavenly love' so beautifully depicted in popular novels.[87] Once again she forcefully stressed the point that there was nothing 'heavenly' in man-woman relationship. It was earthy, of the earth, and there was nothing to be ashamed of this fact of life. As long as a man was not mature enough, old enough for reproduction, he would not feel the urge for this 'heavenly emotion', and it, according to her, went to prove that 'love' basically was nothing but meaningful sexual relationship between two adults of opposite sex.[88]

Kiranmayee, unfortunately, fell victim to the other kind of love, which went beyond mere physical needs, which she visualized to have existed between Upendra and Surobala, love with all its serenity and softness. In her own way Kiranmayee tried to achieve and share it and was contemptuously rejected by Upendra. She was severely censured for her unseemly behaviour with Dibakar, who was put under the guardianship of the lady. Frustration and resentment, along with her hopeless situation, finally engulfed her whole being and at an insane moment she decided to elope with Dibakar, Upendra's protégé. Only in this way, she knew, she could undermine Upendra's authority and inflict on him the most crippling sense of shame. Her nemesis, of course, was quite at hand. Society perceived her as a deviant on more than one count and punitive measures were sure to follow.[89] That was, after all, the vision of social norm, of social justice professed and shared by most of the fiction writers of this period, be it Bankim, Sarat or even Tagore. They had to keep in mind, perhaps, the popular response as well as reaction to whatever they were trying to convey, and could not very well go beyond the limits society imposed upon them. Social deviance, where women were involved, had to be followed by total destruction. 'In literature, as in life, unconventional women needed to be severely punished lest their defiant attitudes inspire further acts of rebellion.'[90] Sarat, in spite of all his compassionate understanding and sympathy for women, had to take recourse to some conventional moral judgements against the 'sins' the society would not condone. In Kiranmayee's case, the punishment came from within—from her own self as well as outside. This 'incomparable beauty' lost her looks which amounts to the loss of femininity, 'just' punishment for a sexual offender. But it appears to be insignificant compared to her ultimate loss of sanity.[91] The loss of her sanity balances the preservation of society's sanity, manifest in its order.

Binodini's action unlike Kiranmayee's showed much finesse. She could no way be termed headstrong or impulsive. She moved in a cool and calculated fashion and designed every step of her scheme cautiously. True, the first seed of rancour and resentment took root because of the fact that once Mahendra, hero of the novel, had rejected the proposal of marriage with her. Then came Binodini's marriage and subsequent widowhood. The picture of blissful conjugal happiness Mahendra and his wife Asha were supposedly enjoying did nothing to assuage this feeling of frustration. Binodini did not intend to impose her presence on Mahendra directly and as the first step towards her ultimate goal (to see Mahendra on his knees), she created space for herself in his household by making herself indispensable to his mother and later striking a pretence of friendship with Asha. Binodini was a widow, but not a child widow. She was married at a comparatively mature age to a completely unworthy person. The death of her husband did not create any emotional crisis in her life. She was a woman of keen intelligence, rare competence and moderate education and not without physical attributes and charm. When she appeared in the midst of a happy and harmonious household of Mahendra and Asha, she was rudely reminded of her physically, emotionally and intellectually deprived life. As a widow, she could never aspire to have the taste of the blissful conjugal drama being enacted around her, which was made clear when she rejected Behari's proposal of marriage on the grounds that such a marriage would never be accepted in society. What made her all the more vengeful was the fact of Mahendra's rejection of her, as a result of which she had to marry a barbaric monkey of a man from Barasat (*Barasater barbar bandar*)[92] and accept banishment to a remote village. This explicit expression of her arrogance along with her vengefulness are intended in a way to establish her 'capacity to redress a lopsided distribution of power between the sexes'.[93]

In the beginning, she maintained a veneer of indifference to Mahendra. But it was obviously carefully contrived to attract and entice him all the more, and she was in no way proven wrong. For her it was supremely ego satisfying (and she was quite egocentric, no doubt) to find Mahendra prepared to desert his 'beloved' wife and his mother for her sake. But her own feelings towards Mahendra were of a ambivalent nature. She considered him responsible for all the misfortunes in her life. She did not know whether to punish the man severely or to present him with her heart and soul.[94]

Not long after, she was introduced to Behari, Mahendra's well-meaning friend, an ardent well-wisher of the family. Behari's all too transparent concern for Asha's welfare, created other complexities in her life. The ambivalence in Behari's attitude towards Binodini quietly reflects the attitude of the contemporary society towards young widows. The young widows had always been handled with caution. Their deprived and innate sexuality—'unharnessed sexual energy'[95] would pose a threat to the carefully maintained balance of power in the society where widows were treated almost like social outcasts. The 'unharnessed sexual energy' of a young widow is entirely a male construction—in that, the restriction is confined to the remarriage of women; men, widowers, are exempt from it. Yet, it is the men who are both attracted to the sexuality of the young widows, as well as feel threatened by it. With modern education and ensuing reform movements, the conditions of the widows created a sense of guilt in the minds of the educated young men like Behari. He was sympathetic towards Binodini, but could not, interestingly, think of any other prospect for her except leading a forlorn existence within the given framework of society. Binodini never appeared before Behari, but he had seen her all the same. She was not a person, he realized, to be casually abandoned in the wilderness of a small village. He was at the same time acutely aware of the threat Binodini's proximity to Mahendra held for Mahendra and Asha. 'The same woman who is a homemaker can turn out to be destructive and prove to be a homebreaker.'[96] Behari could not, at least at that point of time, think of Binodini's remarriage although he once suggested it. But that was more in jest than out of any serious consideration for her future.[97] This ambivalence in a person like Behari becomes all the more significant as one finds in it the reflection of conflicts and clashes of ideas, old and new, that tormented the mind of the age. Later when Behari proposed marriage to Binodini (because of his personal involvement with her), she, in spite of a very explicit expression of her love for and devotion to him, could not accept his proposal because such a marriage would not be taken kindly by the society.[98] How frustrated Vidyasagar was in his assessment of contemporary society will be illustrated from Binodini's story which more or less represented women's situation at that time.

On a different level, is the relationship between *devar* and *bhabhi*—characterized usually by simplicity of texture but sometimes assuming a complexity which tends to defy accepted social norms. In Bengal there exists a special relationship between the sister-in-law and her younger brother-in-law. It is a sort of sweet and sour relationship, overflowing with jokes and teasing on both sides. In this particular relationship people do not bother much about 'this far and no further' boundary line, or overlook the concept of this line. But the lurking fear, the threat underlying any relationship between the opposite sexes can have some serious implications and Kiranmayee in *Charitraheen* echoed the same sentiment.

> But who knows, this innocent relationship, this exchange of jokes might extend beyond the limits of decency and create havoc in the accepted norm and form of the relationships within the family and produce a *Bishabriksha*[99] and create a feeling of inexorable bitterness and destroy the structured edifice of a relationship.[100]

Amal and Charu's relationship in 'Nastaneer'[101] assumed this sort of complexity. Perhaps out of divergent attitudes on the part of the two protagonists it was a complex situation which threatened to disrupt the placid rhythm of life which Charu and her husband had maintained so far. On Amal's part it was a cordial relationship between a *bouthan* and her *thakurpo* blossoming into a friendship between two kindred souls—a relationship which is accepted with a certain amount of graceful indulgence in Bengal and never frowned upon. (Amal was Bhupati's cousin, but in the close knit texture of joint family concept the distinction between a cousin and a brother often gets obliterated.) For Amal it was a nice enjoyable interlude—away from the pressing schedule of study and looking for livelihood. To discover in Charu a rare sensitive soul encouraged him to give expression to his literary ambitions. There was no question of any commitment on his part. For Charu, on the other hand, coming out of her secluded existence and interacting and establishing rapport with an understanding and sensitive mind with whom she could share all her unrealized dreams, was somewhat like opening up a new vista to a whole new world. The discovery of this new world added new dimensions to her very existence. The sudden loss of that world had an absolutely unsettling and traumatic effect on her mind. She felt totally abandoned in Amal's absence and by the lack of response from his side. (Amal had completely withdrawn himself from the scene as the threat of their relationship was on the verge of crossing that 'forbidden frontier'.) The thought of Amal as a married man created a peculiar void in her mind which all her husband's affectionate solicitude failed to fulfil. Obviously this relationship was not confined within the limit of frivolity between two innocent souls and one cannot but be conscious of the undercurrent of something much more basic and primeval—the sexual undertone.

Here was the dreaded possibility of another *bishabriksha* erupting and upsetting the balance of the structured framework of the patriarchal society and family. No author, not even of Tagore's stature, could venture to let the 'deviancy role' of a woman go unpunished.[102] And what in the eyes of the upholders of norms and codes of good behaviour could be more 'deviant' than for a married woman to be in love with another man and that too her brother-in-law. In *Ghare Baire* Nikhilesh had termed his relationship with his sister-in-law as *cirasambandha*, *satyasambandha* and how fondly did he reminisce his childhood association and evoked a very sensitive image of a relationship which, in the Indian context, holds a rare charm; it often transcends the circle of mundane pettiness that is the wont in interpersonal relationships in a joint family structure. After an early marriage, the child bride was transported to her in-laws' family where she would obviously flounder in the sea of unknown faces and there would start her trials and tribulations, often in some unsympathetic atmosphere. In the midst of all this, she would naturally try to establish some meaningful relationship with a member of her husband's family. 'The most significant relative for the newly married woman in her *sasur-bari* (in-laws' house) is her husband's younger brother.'[103]

Nikhilesh recounted their joint venture in the mango grove and about picking raw mangoes and relishing them together.

There is clearly a suggestion of romance here, without transgressing the sexual boundaries. He also acted as a go-between for his sister-in-law and her formidable husband. And in the process established a relationship, *satysambandha*, which went deep into his very being. Not that there were no ups and downs in this long association, but they always remained very close to each other.[104] But even in this idyllic relationship, the latent threat of innocent romance crossing the bounds and turning into something dangerous remained intact. Bimala time and again had hinted at it, complained about her sister-in-law's coquettish behaviour.[105] The underlying assumption has always been the same—a woman is always suspect. To translate a Bengali proverb roughly, 'until and unless a woman's body is burnt to cinders on her funeral pyre, one could not call her a sati'.

In the whole scheme of interpersonal relationships within the family and outside it, what strikes one most forcefully is the perpetually present feeling of mutual empathy between two female characters. The change of perspective about women, what one expected to be present in men, could be seen in women more clearly. They did not, of course go all out to rebel against the system which kept women always in a subservient position. This bond of empathy can be explained in a way that both of them as women were generally victims of an unequal society. 'The conventional sex role distinctions presented more powerful, multiple and overlapping structures in society at large that encouraged women to view one another as peers "par excellence" because of their shared sexual destiny.'[106] In *Bishabriksha*, Suryamukhi turned at the moment of her misfortune to her sister-in-law Kamalmani. When she discovered her husband's infatuation with Kunda, she confided in Kamal and wrote to her 'Would you not come to see us? Do come once; in your presence perhaps I would be able to forget my misery.'[107]

Kamalmani was quite secure in her husband's love and affection. Nonetheless, what was an immediate threat to Suryamukhi might have been a lurking fear in her mind too. After all, taking a second wife while the first was alive was not altogether a forgotten idea. Bishweshwari in *Palli Samaj* was fully conscious of the mortification Rama was suffering from. In spite of all her sympathy for the unfortunate widow, she could not have changed her lot. But that did not stop her from asking some very crucial questions about the real value of rules and codes of conduct to be observed by widows. She expressed her doubts to Ramesh when she explained to him why she was taking Rama along with her.

> After that she told him in a low, very low voice, 'She had no place of her own in this world, son, that is why I am taking her to the last refuge, at the feet of the Gods.[108] I do not know if she would survive there. If she does, I will ask her to find an answer to this perplexing question—why did God send her to this world with such beauty, accomplishments and such a large heart and then banish her out of it without any fault of her own and condemned her to such a miserable existence? Is there something meaningful behind it, a blessing in disguise, or is it just a surrender to the whims of our society?'[109]

The interesting point to note here is that Bishweshwari instead of sitting on judgement or pronouncing any oft quoted homily to Rama, held society responsible for the misfortune of the widows.

The same sort of perceptive insight and compassionate and sympathetic treatment of a much more catastrophic happening we find in Mrinal's handling of Achala's awkward predicament. Here is a woman with unwavering faith in whatever orthodox society wanted women and widows to be, coming to the final rescue of another woman who had committed 'sins' which were absolutely unforgivable in the eyes of the conventional society. After Suresh's death, she was the one who took charge of Achala's old father and Achala when Mahim failed to find a possible way out for his helpless wife.

> 'Achala was looking for some refuge, some sort of an ashram', Mahim told Mrinal, 'and perhaps you would be able to help her seek it out'. Mrinal raised her eyes and fixed them on his face, 'Yes, I would be able to tell her where lies her salvation, her final refuge, but that would be nothing but the echo of whatever you had taught me after all, whatever I have learnt, I learnt from you alone.'[110]

Rajlakshmi in *Shrikanta* showed the same understanding and appreciation of another woman, Abhaya. Abhaya dared to take the most unusual decision to live with the man who sacrificed everything for her sake than to lead a miserable existence with her husband with a co-wife. While Shrikanta was rather critical of

Abhaya's actions and tried to dissuade her, Rajlakshmi expressed her unreserved admiration, bordering almost on reverence. 'Don't you try to judge her actions in a hurry and don't you apply the same scale to measure her sins or virtues as you do about other ordinary women like us.'[111]

This statement of Rajlakshmi appears to be the fallout of the social deprivation she herself had to suffer. Obviously she did not wish the same fate to cast its shadow on Abhaya's existence. If she did not possess enough courage to defy her milieu (thus characterizing herself as an ordinary woman), she nevertheless identified herself with another woman who did. Both Abhaya and Rajlakshmi seemed to have perceived motherhood as the most cherished and valuable asset in a woman's life.[112] For Rajlakshmi, motherhood remained an unfulfilled dream, mainly because of her questionable past and her not so respectable profession as a courtesan. Shrikanta, if not Rajlakshmi, viewed them as something insurmountable in the way of putting the stamp of legitimacy on their relationship.[113] Abhaya, being away from home in a remote Burmese city at least had the possibility of realizing whatever she had expected from life.

In this myriad and multi-faceted discourse of interpersonal relationship what stands out is the apparent helpless surrender of people, both men and women, to religious, societal power and the force of tradition which they as well worshipped. Society or the social codes of conduct always play a decisive role in defining and redefining the course and the contours of relationships in society and in the family. If we intend to take into account the underlying theme of change in the context of the ongoing state of flux at the social and national levels, to our dismay we find that these changes are not conspicuous in the overall picture of traditional relationship patterns. True, all the female characters within our purview were literate and with their limited exposure to the outside world were aware of the social injustice they were subjected to. They, at the same time, accepted the hard facts of life, one of which was to fall in line with the codified, restrictive roles they had to play. Consequently, their protests, if there were any, had always been muted and confined to questioning and expressing doubts about the validity of these norms of behaviour rather than unequivocal defiance of them. Exceptions, of course, were there and we encounter acts of defiance which inevitably entailed disapproval, condemnation and ultimate destruction. More often than not, these instances of defiance ended in a change of conciliatory and conformist moods invariably with some socio-religious undertones involved in it. This very clearly gives credence to the notion of ambiguity and ambivalence inherent in the contemporary reform movements and the women's question as such. Women, realizing that they could not achieve much through defiance, started creating and enlarging in their subtle, imperceptible and unobtrusive ways space for themselves in the familial and related arenas. In the next chapter, we would endeavour to explore the notional, conceptual images of the woman grappling with tension present in the family and in society and extending her influence whichever way it was possible for her.

NOTES AND REFERENCES

1. R.S. Khare, 'From *Kanya* to *Mata*: Aspects of the Cultural Language of Kinship in Northern India', in Akos Oster, Leena Fruzzetti and Steve Barnet, eds., *Concepts of Person: Kinship, Caste and Marriage in India*, New Delhi: OUP, 1992, p. 156.
2. Josodhara Bagchi, 'Presenting Nationalism: Ideology of Motherhood in Colonial Bengal', *Economic and Political Weekly*, 20-7 Oct. 1990.
3. Doranne Jacobson, 'The women of North and Central India: Goddesses and Wives', in Doranne Jacobson and Susan S. Wadley, *Women in India: Two Perspectives*, New Delhi: Manohar, 1977, p. 61.
4. Leela Dube, 'On the Construction of Gender', in Karuna Chanana, ed., *Socialization, Education and Women*, New Delhi: Orient Longman, 1988, p. 180.
5. Sarat Chatterjee, *Palli Samaj*, p. 258.
6. Sarat Chatterjee, *Debdas*, pp. 45-8.
7. Humayun Kabir, *The Bengali Novel*, Calcutta: Firma K.L. Mukhopadhyay, 1968, p. 80.
8. Sarat Chatterjee, *Shrikanta*, p. 519.
9. Ibid., p. 687.
10. Ibid., p. 519.
11. Bankim Chatterjee, *Debichoudhurani*, p. 685.

12. For the Indian concept of pre-pubertal marriage, see Maria Mies, *Indian Women and Patriarchy: Conflicts and Dilemmas of Students and Working Women*, New Delhi: Concept Publishing Company, 1980, pp. 51-2.
13. Sarat Chatterjee, *Arakshania*, p. 346.
14. Sudhir Kakar, *The Inner World: A Psycho-analytic Study of Childhood and Society in India*, New Delhi: OUP, 1992, p. 58.
15. Ibid., p. 355.
16. Tagore, 'Shubha' (short story).
17. Ibid., p. 146.
18. Tagore, 'Dena Paona' (short story).
19. Ibid., pp. 31, 33.
20. Vanaja Dhruvarajan, *Hindu Women and the Power of Ideology*, New Delhi: Vistaar Publication, 1989, p. 38.
21. Sarat Chatterjee, *Gribadaba.*
22. Ibid., pp. 515-16.
23. Ibid., p. 516.
24. Ibid., pp. 584-5.
25. Tagore, 'Haimanti' (short story).
26. Ibid., p. 626.
27. Ibid. In this context one is reminded of Sudhir Kakar's comment in *The Inner World*, 'We should note in passing that the Sita legend also gives us a glimpse into the human imagery of manliness. Rama may have all the traits of a god-like hero, yet he is also fragile, mistrustful and jealous and *very much a conformist, both to his parents' wishes and to social opinion*', p. 66.
28. Ibid., p. 619.
29. Tagore, 'Aparichita' (short story).
30. Ibid., p. 677.
31. See Tanika Sarkar, 'Bengali Women in Politics—The 1920s and 30s', in Kumkum Sangari and Sudesh Vaid, eds., *Women and Culture*, Bombay: SNDT University, 1985, p. 184.
32. Tagore, *Jogajog.*
33. Ethel Spector Parson, 'Sexuality as the Mainstay of Identity: Psycho-analytic Perspectives', in Catherine R. Stimpson and Ethel Spector Parson, eds., *Women, Sex and Sexuality*, Chicago and London: University of Chicago Press, 1980, p. 26.
34. Tagore, *Ghare Baire.*
35. Ibid., pp. 407-8.
36. Ibid.
37. *Laws of Manu*, V: 154, tr. Wendy Doniger, with Brian K. Smith, London: Penguin Classics, 1991.
38. Sarat Chatterjee, *Shrikanta*, p. 412.

39. Ibid.
40. Bankim Chatterjee, *Bishabriksha*, p. 198.
41. Sudhir Kakar, *Intimate Relations: Exploring Indian Sexuality*, New Delhi: Penguin, 1989, p. 66.
42. Ibid., p. 67.
43. Sarat Chatterjee, *Charitraheen.*
44. Ibid., p. 130.
45. Sarat Chatterjee, *Grihadaha,* p. 484.
46. Tagore, 'Didi' (short story).
47. Ibid., p. 275.
48. Ibid., p. 279.
49. Tagore, 'Drishtidaan' (short story).
50. Ibid., p. 395.
51. Ibid., p. 405.
52. Meredith Borthwik, 'The Bhadramahila and Changing Conjugal Relations in Bengal, 1850-1900', in M. Allen and S.N. Mukherjee, *Women in India and Nepal*, Canberra: ANU, 1982, p. 105.
53. Surobala in Sarat's *Charitraheen.* 'She was the domestic incarnation of the new woman, talented, virtuous and beautiful.' Dorothy Ko, *Teachers of the Inner Chamber*, p. 181.
54. Kamal in Sarat's *Sheshprashna.*
55. Kiranmayee in *Charitraheen.*
56. Mrinal in Tagore's 'Streer Patra'.
57. Amongst others, we can name a few luminaries like Swarnakumari Devi, Gyanadanandini Devi and Sarla Debichoudhurani. Also see Ghulam Murhsid, *Reluctant Debutante*, pp. 207-31.
58. Partha Chatterjee, *The Nation and its Fragments: Colonial and Post-Colonial History*, New Delhi: OUP, 1995, p. 128.
59. Ibid., pp. 148-9.
60. Tagore, *Ghare Baire,* p. 475.
61. Ibid.
62. Sarat Chatterjee, *Charitraheen.*
63. 'Patro O Patri' (short story).
64. Ibid., p. 705.
65. Sarat Chatterjee, *Grihadaha.*
66. Tagore, *Ghare Baire.*
67. Humayun Kabir, *The Bengali Novel*, p. 76.
68. Sarat Chatterjee, *Grihadaha*, p. 570.
69. Ibid., p. 592.
70. Ibid., p. 531.
71. Ibid., pp. 491-512.
72. Ibid., p. 575.
73. Tagore, *Ghare Baire*, pp. 478-9.

74. Ibid., p. 479.
75. Ibid.
76. B.B. Majumdar, *Heroines of Tagore: A Study in the Transformation of Indian Society 1875-1941*, Calcutta: Firma K.L. Mukhopadhyaya, 1968, p. 248.
77. Tagore, *Ghare Baire*, p. 491.
78. Ibid.
79. 'Like a pampered fish in a bowl, I have always swum in the water created specially for me', ibid., p. 554. This statement of Bimala precisely presents the image of privileged upper class *bhadramahila* nurtured with care, nonetheless in seclusion, in a specific milieu preordained by the upper class society.
80. Ibid., p. 475.
81. Ibid., p. 513.
82. Ibid.
83. Sarat Chatterjee, *Gribadaha*, p. 605.
84. Sarat Chatterjee, *Charitraheen*, p. 231.
85. Ibid., p. 163.
86. Ibid.
87. Ibid., p. 252.
88. Ibid.
89. See S.F. Nadel, *The Theory of Social Structure*, London: Cohen and West, 1957, for a theoretical discussion of deviancy roles.
90. Lisa Leiberman, 'Crimes of Reason, Crimes of Passion: Suicide and adulterous woman in nineteenth-century France', *Journal of Family History*, vol. 24, no. 2, April 1999, p. 133.
91. *Charitraheen*, p. 334.
92. Tagore, *Chokher Bali*, p. 261.
93. Sudhir Kakar, *Intimate Relations: Exploring Indian Sexuality*, New Delhi: Penguin, 1989, p. 13.
94. Ibid., p. 251.
95. Meenakshi Mukherjee, *Realism and Reality: The Novel and Society in India*, New Delhi: OUP, 1985, p. 70.
96. *Chokher Bali*, p. 238.
97. Ibid.
98. Ibid., p. 373.
99. Bankim's *Bishabriksha* became a reference point wherever there was the slightest possibility of a deviant relationship.
100. *Charitraheen*, p. 249. Sudhir Kakar in his *Intimate Relations* has talked about this relationship in the north Indian context, 'Expressed in a certain tenderness, in erotically tinged banter or cases of actual physical intimacy, the relationship is very much part of marriage's emotional space', p. 13.

101. Tagore, 'Nashtaneer' (short story).
102. Nadel, op. cit., pp. 49-50.
103. Manisha Roy, *Bengali Women*, Chicago: University of Chicago Press, 1975, p. 106.
104. For a detailed discussion of *devar-bhabhi* relationship, see M. Roy, op. cit., pp. 106-10. The author has discussed why this relationship does not usually assume a sexual overtone.
105. *Ghare Baire*, p. 477.
106. Nancy F. Cott, *The Bonds of Womanhood: 'Women's Sphere' in New England, 1780-1835*, New Haven and London: Yale University Press, 1977, p. 188.
107. *Bishbriksha*, p. 194.
108. It was a very old custom in Bengal where widows, young or old, were shunted off to some holy place of pilgrimage, especially Varanasi, Mathura-Vrindavan and Puri to avoid physical, social and moral responsibility involved in looking after them.
109. Sarat Chatterjee, *Palli Samaj*, p. 268.
110. *Grihadaha*, p. 606.
111. *Shrikanta*, p. 514.
112. Ibid.
113. Meenakshi Mukherjee, op. cit., p. 122.

CHAPTER 3

Women's Power and Space

The exploration here is based on the assumption that each human being, in our case women, creates and enlarges space for oneself within the confines of one's location. The emerging middle class and its ethos made the existential limits of life's passage all the more irksome for women, much more than for the men. Men, of course, tried to shrug off the inherited burden with much greater energy, in an assertive sort of way. Women, unable to break out of the confines, physical, social or moral, completely, started making room for themselves, stretching the limits a slight bit here, a little bit there, and in the process to enlarge the circle of their activity considerably. The strategies adopted for this would vary from one context to another, indeed from one person to another, and the range of these would extend from utter conformity to the given norm, sly subversion through deception or flattery, and open defiance. Even passive conformity, which has been termed 'wise passiveness', to the norm of *patibratya*, and good motherhood had its victories, earning for the woman a space that bordered on the family's respect and therefore a degree of empowerment: the power that a young wife would exercise over her husband through either the denial or the giving of access to her body; the power of a fecund mother over the household even as her own sexual appeal receded.

Once an amicable relationship is developed, the wife may suggest and remind her husband of various things to be done. . . . To get her own way, she may use feminine wiles like crying, fasting and gradually learning to recognize her husband's idiosyncrasies and developing strategies to manipulate him.[1]

True, the strategies the women adopted were confined within the given structure of power relations, within 'women's historically limited spheres of power',[2] but it is precisely here that we find their ingenuity in accommodating themselves in a more meaningful sense without overthrowing the hierarchical structure of authority. More often than not, women derive immense power out of 'abject' conformity to the accepted social, moral or religious norms. And this power obviously equips the woman to enlarge her space and legitimize her position in the family as well as in the immediate social community. 'Some [women] undoubtedly found that behaving in accordance with the ideal gained them certain advantages, including protection and support, as well as a measure of social respect.'[3]

The example of this we find in the case of Suryamukhi in Bankim's *Bishabriksha* who was a self-confessed *patibrata* and consequently her sexual chastity and fidelity were above suspicion. These have been instrumental in lending her an aura of sublimity, of power, and when she came back home after a long absence, during which time her whereabouts were absolutely unknown to the people concerned, she discovered her husband thoroughly grief-stricken and full of self-reproach. Yet, so secure was he in her inviolable fidelity that the question of any suspicion did not even vaguely appear in his mind, nor in the minds of the other inmates of the house, even the neighbours, who all merely rejoiced at her return. Even imagining that she could have compromised her chastity was beyond the realm of the possible.[4]

The Indian woman established her chastity as an undeniably important 'fact' and by doing so recognized the 'supreme importance of her own position'.[5] 'Hence all encompassing joy rather than gloom, greets her return.'[6]

In *Debichoudhurani* Bankim has been accused of conforming to convention when he allowed Prafulla to give up her role of the leader of a religio-political group and accept her ascribed position as one of the three wives of her husband. 'It is thus a strain on the readers' credulity when we are asked to believe that she finds fulfilment and satisfaction in becoming one of the many wives of Brajeshwar in a thoroughly conventional and domesticated [*sic*] family.'[7] Perhaps this sort of accusation itself conforms to the convention of locating meanings at the surface of the text. Prafulla, none too ignorant or weak a person, had always shown the capacity of taking her own decisions.[8] It was, therefore, a wilful assertion of a choice on her part to return to her husband's house after a gamut of 'masculine' experiences. The virtual anonymity of her two co-wives juxtaposed to her own centrality to the whole story almost wipes them out as contenders for the husband's affection as well as from the story's space; they are not ones she would perhaps even take note of in determining her relationship with her husband. Whatever attention her husband gave to her co-wives was due to her own constant reminders of his responsibilities towards them. Indeed, even the husband's own role in this determination gets subordinated to her will. All this, even as she conformed to convention. In her own way Prafulla followed the norms of a devoted wife, even at the cost of defying her mentor, Bhawani Pathak. For example, when she was practising austerity in the use of food, clothes and bodily comforts, she stuck to the ritual of eating fish on the day of *Ekadashi*.[9] Even before becoming the dreaded Debichoudhurani, Prafulla was more than willing to accept her position as one of the three wives of her husband. True, later in her life, she had a glorious choice, an alternative before her. But didn't she reject that alternative consciously and after much deliberation? She perhaps intended to seek out her life's fulfilment in the role of a wife and a mother in a thoroughly 'conventional and domesticated family' and create space there only for herself. When she ceased to rule over the band of *santans* who were used as the instrument of bringing about social justice by her and her mentor Bhawani Pathak, she assumed the leadership role in her husband's household making her once hostile in-laws to literally eat out of her hand. And this is how she vindicated and legitimized her role and her position.[10]

Mrinal's 'power', on the other hand, lay in conforming to the ideal image of a self-sacrificing and self-effacing young widow and that is how she transformed her desolate and forlorn existence into something useful and beneficial and derived power out of her self-abnegation. This image is, no doubt, suited to the orthodoxy of society which imposed severe restrictions on the life of a widow. At the same time it gives women some scope to alter their mode of living, if only just a wee bit in the otherwise all encompassing atmosphere of deprivation and severely limited existence. First Mrinal made herself useful to her elderly husband and old mother-in-law; then after their demise, she took Achala's father under her wing and rendered help and support to him in full measure. She assumed Achala's role and scored a point over her; her asexual and chaste way of life attracted respect and admiration, even from a person like Suresh, which was eloquently illustrated by his outburst against Achala when he was about to go on a journey with her, without the knowledge of her husband, and presuming her compliance. Observing her consternation and dismay, he lashed out: 'The look of shocked innocence does not suit you Achala, it would have suited Mrinal. A crow might borrow peacock's feathers and adorn itself, but that would not hide its true image.'[11]

This image of a self-effacing, young widow is clearly a pre-eminently male construction, true to the tradition of a patriarchal social setting. It echoes, interestingly, the arguments put forward by Raja Rammohun Roy against *satidaha* and in favour of widows engaged in *nishkama karma*, leading an ascetic life.[12] Mrinal no doubt transformed all her deprivations into resources and created a very valuable space for herself in her immediate social circle. It was, after all, better than leading a secluded life with a shaven head and having a meal once in a day in complete isolation. 'Although women could not rewrite the rules that structured their lives, they were extremely creative in crafting a space from within the prevailing gender system that gave them meaning, solace and dignity.'[13] Achala's encounter with another absolutely tradition-bound ordinary woman once again reinforced the idea of how successfully women within the restricted confines of their home and in spite of their subservient status could extend their power base by keeping a strict control over their husbands and their activities. 'When she was waiting on her husband and attending to his needs, she considered herself a slave—a *dasi.* But in other domestic matters she was the supreme authority in the household, she was the one who ordered her husband around.'[14] Simone de Beauvoir too is sensitive to women's sly empowerment through apparent conformity. She observes: 'By making herself a slave, she has found the surest means of enchaining him.'[15]

Bijoya, in Sarat's *Datta*, an educated and enlightened Brahmo girl, did not feel constrained to express similar sentiments when she pointed out that Indian women would not even think of eating with their menfolks, whatever might be the women's status in society. They would prefer to look after the needs of the men with loving care and consider it a blessing to be able to do so. She continued in the same vein and said that through these mundane chores like serving and tending to the requirements of men at their mealtime women exert their power and influence over them.[16]

If Mrinal could extend her domain by virtue of her sympathetic understanding of human character and her selfless support and service to others, Surobala's power lay in her vulnerable innocence, her guileless faith in all things traditional and in her indefatigable defence of it all. Her unquestioning trust in, and dependence on, her husband made him, in his turn, rely on her entirely. Upendra also exhibited very high esteem for his wife when he told Dibakar that if his (Dibakar's) wife was half as beautiful and had half of Surobala's qualities of head and heart, any husband should consider himself immensely fortunate.[17] Upendra could not think of an existence without Surobala. Satish cited an example to show to Kiranmayee how Upendra had arranged everything for the marriage of one very dear friend and follower of his, but did not attend the wedding as Surobala was unwell. He spent the whole evening attending to his wife's needs in the face of earnest requests and remonstrations from all and sundry.[18] The whole episode revived in Kiranmayee the feeling of utter loneliness that encompassed her own existence. She could not for a moment recollect the memory of any such moment of tenderness which could sustain her. 'Kiranmayee stared silently like a statue. In the depth of her inner self, gnawing along the dark corners, she tried to pull out a moment like that but failed.'[19]

A woman like Kiranmayee, proud, self-willed and self-confident, accepted defeat and recognized Surobala as her superior, her guru.[20]

The search for the women's creation and enlargement of space for themselves, must, however, compel the memory of socially prescribed roles they are expected to act out. For such roles establish a social order and legitimize its functioning.[21]

Subversion of male authority has always been a means through which women have tried to assert themselves and thus enlarge their own space. This subversion is sometimes physical, at others it might be symbolic. And this act of subversion covers a whole range of human behaviour, from the mundane to the sublime. Nowhere could we find a more compelling or more pronounced example of subversion of societal as well as individual authority as in the case of Kiranmayee's final act of defiance. It is a physical subversion of society's norms and the individual authority of Upendra's when she took Dibakar along on a desperate journey to an unknown land. Binodini also successfully undermined male domination and male ego by making Mahendra grovel before her and then quietly transferring her loyalty to Behari. This way she subverted the social norm as well as the individual norms of behaviour. To what end, of course, is a much debatable point but she had the fortitude to take her own decision and stick by it which is the ultimate testimony to the realization of one's self-identity.

Mrinal in 'Streer Patra'[22] or Anila in 'Poila Number'[23] subverted the concept of inescapable male protection and domination in a more subtle and symbolic way. Mrinal refused to go back to her husband's house, to its restrictive, inhibitive ambience and tried to seek out a life away from it all. Mrinal had already created space for herself by being 'different' from others, by virtue of having qualities which are associated more commonly with masculinity. 'I was beautiful, but you could dismiss and overlook that quite easily. What you were forever conscious of and what made you ever so uncomfortable was my intelligence.'[24]

Subversion might take countless different forms. For Bindu,

Mrinal's surrogate daughter in 'Streer Patra', courting death itself was an escape from normative order which dictated her to remain a devoted wife to her insane husband; the escape was also tinged with defiance. As Mrinal says, 'Bindu was just a woman, and everyone treated her as such, but God at least did not deprive her of his benediction'.[25] The space she created was through a repudiation of life itself, for life had denied her a personal space thrice over in all the milestone rites of passage. In her life after death, Mrinal felt, her being was sublimated and she was merged in the eternity of life, 'where she was not only an unfortunate female child in a traditional Bengali family, nor an unwelcome burden on her grudging and unwilling guardians, nor a badly deceived wife of an insane husband; there she has been able to merge with eternity'.[26]

Parbati in *Debdas* tried to subvert social norms (although in her case it was more symbolic than tangible) when she expressed her intention to take Debdas along with her to her husband's house. Her friend was scandalized, '"How could you have done that, it would have been such a shame." Parbati remained unperturbed, "What shame? I'm taking my own thing along with me, why should that be shameful?"'[27]

Parbati's space arose from conformity to the norms of behaviour laid down by orthodox Hindu society. 'My own thing' is an interesting metaphor used by a woman for her man, an inversion of the 'proprietary' right of a man over a woman sanctioned by marital custom; the inversion is all the more emphatic, for Parbati is asserting her 'proprietary' right over a man she had chosen for herself, rather than one assigned to her by society through the ritual of marriage. But then this inversion remained symbolic, for she did reconcile herself to her role as the wife of the man she had to accept and there arises the more fundamental question. This seemingly daring inversion is just a cosmetic gesture which is ever so easily smothered by patriarchy's manifold manoeuvring in the name of family honour. At the end of the story when Parbati comes to know about Debdas' sordid death and rushes out of her house to have a last look at Debdas, her husband and her stepson stop her, to keep their family name and prestige intact. A much more daring and innovative mode of subversion we find in Giribala, heroine of

Tagore's 'Manbhanjan'.[28] When Giribala, failed to win back her wayward husband by deploying familiar 'feminine wiles like crying, fasting',[29] etc., and could not stop him from embarking on a pleasure trip along with one of the well-known actresses of the local stage, a theatre addict herself, she found a wonderful opening to turn all the social diktats upside down by joining the stage herself. The story ends with Giribala, in all her glory, standing under the arc lights, head held high, and the audience applauding while her husband screamed murder from the floor of the theatre.[30] She, the dominated housewife, stood at centre stage then, the agent of a veritable upheaval in the world constituted by the two halves—the stage and the audience, one the active subject of the upheaval, the other the passive spectator. The personal discomfiture of the husband, standing aghast in the audience, was submerged in the collective applause and approval, of that symbolic inversion. He did try to assert his identity by 'screaming murder', the identity of the husband being betrayed by the wife, but who could still establish his dominance by screaming; but, his lone voice, being drowned out in the deafening applause, and her triumphal and unperturbed presence on the stage only highlighted his helplessness. The loss of his own identity to that of his wife, the cynosure of all eyes, was the exact opposite of the roles within the precincts of the household. This defiance and this defeat of conventional social norms, the acts by which she tried to demolish the concept of superior male authority and supremacy, do not always take such dramatic shape or come out so forcefully. Kamal in *Sheshprashna* in her own way and in what she thought was a rational and pragmatic fashion, challenged all the 'time honoured' and 'tradition bound' formats of hierarchical human relationships and tried to put them in a somewhat feminist perspective. She very openly questioned the wisdom of accepting everything received and did so in the face of stiff male opposition. While admiring the beauty of the Taj Mahal, she remained unimpressed by the theory of Shah Jahan's single-minded devotion to his wife. 'But did he not have other wives too? He might have loved Mumtaz a little more than others, but it was not in any way unflinching devotion to one person only.'[31]

Her equally defiant utterances about the fate of widows and

codes of conduct expected of them shocked the other members of the group, mainly male members. They were waxing eloquent about how the unfortunate widows of Hindu society led a life of total and unblemished purity, only with the memory of their late husbands to sustain them. Kamal ruthlessly cut them short asserting that it was an absolute myth and a male construction. She was willing to accept it if they admitted that it was given the garb of truth only to deceive the widows. Kamal's blunt assertions of her impressions put her male acquaintances immediately on the defensive and her statements were branded 'immoral' as well as 'obscene'.[32] Kamal was a threat to their world-view and their dominant status.

If we perceive subversion as formidable only at the hands of the unconventional and out of the ordinary characters, we would fall short of appreciating the intrinsic complexity of this kind of manoeuvre.

> The structuring of women as a gendered subject (through Hindu rituals and practices) is fundamentally implicated in the constitution and reproduction of a social system characterised by the subordination of women. To state this, however, is not to argue that women are passive, unquestioning victims of these practices and representations of these practices. It is to suggest that Hindu rituals and practices set certain limits in terms of the disposition they inculcate among women and different kinship roles with varying status which they assign to them within the family. The rituals and practices and the social system are, moreover, imbued with a certain givenness and appear as a part of the natural order of things. It is within these limits that women question their subordination, express resentment, use manipulative strategies, often against other women in the family, carve out living space and collude in their own oppression.[33]

In the sphere of mundane domestic matters women from within their secluded and sheltered existence often subvert male authority, sometimes openly, at other times by subterfuge and carve out a living space for themselves. 'Indeed one may be tempted to argue that when the line between hostile environment and favourable is drawn close to the front door, the importance of the home and the status of the woman inside, as its symbol and guardian becomes correspondingly greater.'[34] Mothers of grown-up sons wield considerable power in family affairs, particularly in the matters of children's marriages and things pertaining to them.[35] 'Once an amicable relationship is developed, the wife may suggest and remind her husband of various things to be done . . .'[36] or even issue some explicit or implicit orders as happens in Sarat's *Parineeta*. Nabin Roy, Shekhar's father, a hard-headed, pragmatic businessman was quite helpless before his wife. He might fret and fume privately but could not overrule his wife's diktat about Shekhar's marriage. Nabin Roy tried to get his son married to the daughter of a moneyed man and was about to finalize the deal. But his wife sent a message that unless and until Shekhar had seen and approved of the girl, the marriage proposal should not be finalized. 'Nabin Roy, on that day had his midday meal quite late and had his afternoon nap in the outer quarters.'[37] That was all left to him to express his disapproval of her dominance. One is here reminded of Sudhir Kakar's perceptive observation on interpersonal relationships and status of women in the context of strict hierarchy of patriarchal Indian society.

> The outstanding example of the discrepancy between traditional norm and actuality of daily life is the common fact that the powerful role played by the older women in the family—mothers and grandmothers—bears little resemblance to the Hindu ideal of the deferential '*pativrata*' (everloyal to her husband) wife. . . . Although the wife of the family patriarch may indeed pay a formal, and often perfunctory deference to her husband, especially in front of strangers, she may exercise considerable domestic power, not merely among the other women of the household, but with her husband, and she often makes many of the vital decisions affecting the family's interests.[38]

Brajeshwar's mother in *Debichoudhurani* in the same simple and straightforward way took the decision about him and Prafulla when Brajeshwar brought her back after an absence of ten years. She silenced her husband with some well argued comments and the final threat of suicide if he refused to accept Prafulla back. And the father had to acquiesce. Bankim himself preferred to elaborate the implications: 'We will have to accept that the mistress of the house showed rare skill in handling things. A house, like a boat, with such a navigator, will always be able to steer clear of all problems.'[39]

We must remind ourselves over again of the socially prescribed roles for women as we attempt to capture their exploration of personal space. A society assigns some normatively formulated gender roles for the maintenance of its order, i.e. its existing power structure. This system, it is assumed, favours

> the construction of a social identity by complex sets of often unconscious processes, which make the identity seem 'natural' and give the constructions their plausibility. Like the processes whereby a differentiated identity is constructed in girls and boys through the various stages from infancy to adolescence. They are the ones through which children develop qualities, attitudes and capacities, learn patterns of behaviour, form desires and expectations that are appropriate to their adult gender roles and their relationships with the opposite sex.[40]

Within the carefully circumscribed domain of power, in the restricted sphere of female existence monitored by the laws of patriarchy, one would expect women, particularly of the period and milieu of our study, to stick to the images or roles handed down to them by a relationship structure basically orthodox and with hierarchical regimentation. But surprisingly, here we find quite a few characters—from the sublime to the ordinary, to have accepted the role of leadership, or at least of commanding authority quite easily and vindicating themselves in a convincing manner. Role reversal, in this sense, does not in any way mean abandoning the notion of femininity and being oblivious of feminine duties and obligations. It is, on the other hand, the blending of both where women of exceptional qualities assume some 'masculine' attributes and successfully occupy 'supposedly masculine' roles for an effective challenge to be mounted upon the assumed naturalness of gender characteristics.[41] This empowerment of the female self is met with approval in society as long as the power was engaged in improving the quality of life in their immediate surrounding and making it their primary concern. We have repeatedly observed these 'contradictory pulls' in the Bengali *bhadralok* consciousness of this period—'a fascination for the empowered female and a simultaneous compulsion to harness the threatening energy into safe, socially sanctioned roles'.[42] It is thus that Debichoudhurani had to appear at the end of the story as Prafulla once again. In spite of recognizing in her the incarnation of 'the evil-destroying Krishna, *paritranaya sadhunam vinashaya cha dushkritam; dharmasansthapanaya hetuh sambhavami yuge yuge*',[43] Bankim did not allow her to go out in the open battlefield to destroy the enemy. Prafulla was made to appear to have happily devoted all her energy and expertise to promoting the welfare and prosperity of her family and the community around her. She even declared that ruling over a band of outlawed bandits was not a woman's job,[44] thus succumbing to the normative construction of gender roles that she had so triumphantly transcended. But for all practical purposes right from protecting her in-laws' social prestige to saving her husband's life, even if we were to forget her role as the leader of a group of good Samaritans, all out to help people in need, she was the protector, the saviour, a role traditionally assumed by men. Here quite obviously role reversal was complete, in defiance of societal norms. Prafulla in the end had to revert to the stereotypical role of a wife and mother, and enlarge her base of power and seek out her space in the socially sanctioned sphere of the family, even if she did so of her own will and on her own terms. No doubt she could leave a distinctive mark on the things she was involved with and her strong, forceful personality did not fail to create an impression on the people around her. But the role reversal and defiance were transient, a passing moment yielding to the prescriptive norm, which, by contrast, assumed the characteristics of being eternal.

On the other hand, Mrinal's character in 'Streer Patra' juxtaposed against Prafulla's brings into focus the fundamental difference in their individual perspectives on their roles in the family and in society. Whereas Prafulla accepted the predominant norms in the end, Mrinal's approach had always been marked with questioning the validity and sanctity of the system. She created space for herself in the humdrum routine and insensitive way of life in her in-laws' household on the strength of her individuality, her non-conformity and her keen intelligence—which always caused some discomfort among the people around her. 'My mother was perpetually worried about it, for women it was such a nuisance. Intelligence for one who all her life has to accept control from above, would be the cause of final destruction.'[45]

For a woman to be intelligent was inexcusable as it was a threat to male superiority. Women have always been portrayed as weak not only in body, but in mind too. Mrinal, in her attempt to save and protect the life and honour of Bindu, committed a much more grievous offence. She could not have changed the system, she knew, not even have given it a furious shake; what she wanted to do was to register her protest by taking the unfortunate girl along with her and decide about her future away from the ever forbidding and censuring crowd. When she failed, she decided to opt out, to withdraw from the unfeeling structure. She realized how futile it was to fight it and even the death of an innocent girl could not make any dent on its sepulchrous exterior. Her acceptance of defeat, but not the indignity of surrender, was yet an act of defiance. Her departure from accepted norm was complete when she ended her letter by severing her familial relationship and thereby discovering a new ray of hope—hope of her survival.[46]

A striking facet which emerges from the notion of inversion is that the occasional assumption of male roles by women does not in any way dispossess them of their femininity.[47] If the patriarchal hierarchy imposed categorically differentiated gender roles, women's subversion, inversion, questioning of these roles did not conform to the counterposition, did not appropriate the one by giving up the other; on the contrary, it created shades of ambiguity between the two categories. This ambiguity gave women a power which was for ever beyond the reach of men as in the case of Mrinal in *Gribadaba*. She assumed the responsibility of uniting Achala's father with her, and not only did she venture out of her home and come to Calcutta, but even undertook the journey to Dihri in Bihar, itself a considerable step on the part of a young widow from a small village. What distinguishes her all the more is her confidence when she asserted that she would very well be able to find for Achala a way out of her dilemma. And all this, without for a moment being forgetful of her 'womanly duties'. It is this perhaps which has been called 'the hidden power of women'.[48]

One can observe the same 'hidden power' manifest in Kalyani in Tagore's short story 'Aparichita'. In the first part of the story, Kalyani remained a disembodied, invisible entity, and it was her father who occupied centre stage in asserting his identity and his individuality. While sending away the wedding party without solemnizing the wedding, he did not seem to have taken his daughter's opinion into consideration. One can imagine her as a distant shadowy figure, waiting anxiously for a charmed life and then suddenly waking up to its hard realities. The second half of the story, clearly meant as a counterposition to the first, is focussed on the male protagonist's chance encounter with her in a railway compartment. He was instantly fascinated by the uninhibited demeanour of the girl. But so far she was a half-child, half-woman, acting playfully with the children travelling with her. Very soon the situation came to a head with the arrival of a group of European passengers accompanying a high official, and the station master insisting that they vacate the compartment immediately. Our hero, ready to comply, started collecting his baggage and was about to move out. But some surprise was in store for him. The girl, now totally transformed from an innocent adolescent to an upright assertive individual, stood her ground and put up a stiff resistance. She firmly asked our hero not to stir from his seat, and turned her blazing glance to the station master, challenging his statement about the compartment being a reserved one, and flung the reservation slips pasted by railway employees on to the platform.

> In the meantime the uniformed officer along with his orderly appeared there. He was about to board the train but looking at the girl and listening to her, he changed his mind and conferred with the station master, some distance away. After that, what really happened I do not know, but following the departure schedule, the train resumed its onward journey, with an extra bogey attached to it. The girl immediately reverted to her jesting, joking self; only I had to look out of the window, smarting under the burden of an unbearable sense of shame.[49]

The above episode emphasizes two points cogently and forcefully vis-à-vis the notion of inversion—one, as here, the role reversal was complete as it had been reinforced by the presence of a sense of shame in the man and secondly that women could, with perfect ease, discard their masculine stance and resume their familiar role with the usual elan.

Role reversal, however, was not without its poignantly ironic turns, as we see it in Tagore's *Ghare Baire.* Witnessing the widening chasm in the relationship between Bimala and Nikhilesh, and the presence of an outside factor causing the rift, Nikhilesh's sister-in-law was reminded of similar circumstances in her own life. There was but a small difference: here the familiar miseries and misfortunes generally associated with women's lives are presented in an inverted order. It was now time for the men to suffer, instead of the women. Bimala herself was amazed at the change that had come over her after the arrival of Sandeep in her life.

> Where was my sense of shame at that time, I wondered. I had no time to analyse my actions. My days, my nights were moving around with the speed of a whirlwind. Nothing could penetrate it, not even my feeling of shame. Once my sister-in-law commented, 'So long, Nikhilesh, it was the women in this house who had to shed tears; now it is time for you to cry and suffer, and better be prepared for it.' And then she cast a glance at me, at the effort I had made to appear attractive [before going out to see Sandeep].[50]

Here the repudiation of role reversal is quite clear. Bimala's sister-in-law could not see anything good coming out of the inversion of accepted, normative behaviour on the part of Bimala. She had suffered immensely because of her husband's deviant behaviour when he was alive but that did not, obviously, give her the authority to challenge the system, the structure of relationships which defined women's roles very carefully and put the stamp of irreversibility on them. By being sarcastic about Bimala, she was not only giving vent to her pent-up frustrations, but her disapproval of Bimala's assumption of 'masculine' attributes too. Bimala herself subscribed to the same perception as is evident from her above-cited utterances and consequently, this reversal could never be established as final.

If assuming effective authority in the domestic sphere amounts to 'inversion or reversal of roles', because, after all, 'the domestic sphere cannot be abandoned to women without any control',[51] then in Asha in *Chokher Bali*, we find a most unlikely example of this phenomenon. The magnitude of her personal tragedy, perhaps transformed her from a naive, innocent girl-bride to a commanding, self-assured householder. She was deserted by her husband in favour of another woman. The humiliation involved in it must have been heart-rending, but that did not provoke her to abandon all her duties and responsibilities which devolved upon her in her husband's absence. It, on the other hand, provided her with a rare sense of power and self-possession and also had given her a distinct identity. For no longer was she a puppet following all the whimsical commands of her husband without protests. She was now a self-assured individual with a clear sense of purpose in her demeanour and action. Even her husband was amazed at her transformation.

> Asha had taken over the responsibility of the household with such perfect ease. How simply and effortlessly she asked Mahendra not to enter his ailing mother's bedroom, without the slightest bit of diffidence or resentment on her part. Mahendra was, thus, denied any authority or 'power' in his own house. He had to stand outside his mother's room with his burden of guilt, and wait.[52]

How true the following observation made by Michelle Perrot sounds in this context: 'Domestic heroines, with their suffering, sacrifices and virtue restore the harmony of the household and family peace. They had the power and the duty—to do good.'[53]

And by 'doing good' Asha carved her niche, her special space in the household and in her husband's heart, which one can perceive in Mahendra's unqualified admiration for his wife and in admission of his guilt. The admission of guilt on the part of Mahendra is of pivotal importance here and proves to be a turning point in their relationship. Asha is now an *empowered* woman, deriving her authority from her conscious effort to 'do good' to others. The foregrounding of her husband's guilt and his sense of shame, on the other hand legitimates the power and authority assumed by her in her husband's absence and in his household. This, in its turn, created the other Asha who could establish her moral authority over her guilty husband ever so confidently.

If absolute firmness of character and conviction and

unwavering fortitude are qualities usually associated with male characters, then these are the very qualities in Anandamayee (in *Gora*) that attribute to her the uniqueness which is not very easily discernible in other similar characters or situations. Anandamayee's inversion of role was substantial enough to give her the decisive momentum in all significant locations within the family. It is she who took the decision of adopting Gora as their son.[54] Once again, when her husband was suffering from spiritual mortification because of his past follies, including having the son of a *bidharmi* around and was living in self-imposed exile, Anandamayee remained absolutely unperturbed in the face of opposition from both her husband and the same son. She never lost the equanimity of her character and her steadfast faith in truth. She knew she could never disown Gora just for his parents' religion; her equanimity about differences of religion arising out of Gora's situation encompassed other human beings as well, including her Christian ayah.

> When one looks at a child and embraces it, one realises that it doesn't come to this world carrying the badge of its religion along with it. And I have realised it and then onward I knew if I loathed anyone for being of lower caste or a Christian, God would not forgive me and take you (Gora) away from me.[55]

In Anandamayee, we encounter a rare nobility of character, a breadth of vision which embraced the whole world as her own and these are the qualities which we commonly associate with the other sex. How correctly Gora had visualized in her the image of the country: 'You have no caste or creed, nor do you condemn any one or hate anyone—you are just the image of benevolence and graciousness; you are my country, my India.'[56]

On the other hand, her husband, a highly educated man, much travelled and much exposed to the outside world, remained content in the cocoon of the strict observance of religious rituals and rigid adherence to customs and conventions. Inadvertently, perhaps, she was also inverting another assigned role: that of a female confined to the household versus the other pertaining to the world outside. It was not through her experience away from home and in the wide world that she was able to take decisive stands vis-à-vis her husband and her son; she did so through her inner conviction born of carrying out very traditional roles—that of a mother, steeped in a sense of *dharma*, being counterposed here to the rituals of denominational religion. Being reminded by her husband of her obligations to the society, the community she was born in, she made her stand amply clear: 'Having raised Gora since the day he was born as my son, if I now start following the dictates and injunctions laid down by society, I might please the people around me, but my 'dharma' would not remain intact.'[57]

Dharma for her was not sectarian observance of some formal rites and ceremonies. It was rather to remain true to one's own self, to one's conscience and here lay the fundamental difference between Anandamayee's religiosity and her husband's religion. To encounter such a person, a middle-aged housewife in the middle class milieu, definitely raises questions about the universality of the stereotypical image of woman bogged down in the mire of trivialities, trampled upon and turned into pulp by the unjust system. Injustice, no doubt, was there, and so were the trivialities of life; at the same time women occasionally acquired the power to rise above them all and assert their identity. If women are visualized only as silent sufferers, their inherent individuality will remain unrecognized. 'These women had done the best they could in creating meaning and dignity from within space allotted to them. To mourn their ignorance or condemn a system that represented them without recognizing their pride and satisfaction is to ignore the most essential feature of the women's lives. . . .'[58] Women, prostitutes and 'fallen' women, removed from the centre of society, at its margins, also endeavour to create space for themselves. Their effort aims at gaining social respectability in mainstream society. To achieve this they were expected to sacrifice a lot and their sacrifices often remained unrewarded. Contemporary society was not prepared to condone transgressions on the part of a woman easily.

It will perhaps be in order to recall a distinction recently made between two terms, the prostitute and the 'fallen' woman. According to Lynda Nead:

> The connotation of prostitution were activated through a particular language. Within this system, two terms in particular demand some

consideration; these are the 'prostitute' and the 'fallen' woman. The prostitute connoted a public practice, the regular exchange of sex for money . . . the term 'fallen' woman activated significantly different associations. To begin with, the notion of 'fall' implied that she had been respectable but had dropped out of respectable society.[59]

Chandramukhi in *Debdas* was a woman who could be categorized as a prostitute—one who accepted money for the services rendered.[60] She had no pretence, no claim to respectability or respectable life. But what transformed her from a common courtesan to a simple village woman with very limited means was her love for Debdas. On their first meeting, Debdas felt a strong sense of revulsion towards her and did not even try to hide it from her; quite openly he said, 'How repulsive and how ugly you look', as she was smoking her hookah. When he sneered at her for taking money in exchange of her service Chandramukhi expressed her helplessness.

When asked about it she said, 'Yes, I do take money, otherwise how can I survive?' 'Leave that part alone, I don't want to hear all the details.' Saying so, Debdas took some money out of his pocket and thrust it into her hands and walked out. Chandramukhi wanted to give that money back to Debdas but then she felt hesitant and perhaps not a little scared of this unusual character. And women like her in any way, were quite used to such humiliation and harsh words, so she stood there silently as Debdas went down the stairs.[61]

Afterwards Debdas's perception of her changed and his revulsion was transformed into a sense of grateful affection; but even then he, a social outcast himself, could not think of giving a permanent shelter to this woman. When Debdas decided to go to a place in western India to recoup his failing health, Chandramukhi offered to go with him. '"Let me go with you, you'd at least need a maid there." But Debdas was absolutely outraged at the suggestion; "No, that is impossible. I can't indulge in such a shameful act."'[62]

He, of course, promised a brighter prospect for them in his next life: 'If we meet again after our death, I will never be able to keep away from you.'[63] Chandramukhi mirrored the social perception of a prostitute's fate and demonstrated how she had internalized it perfectly when she felt that if Debdas got any pleasure out of her company—if she could be of any service to him—that should be enough, but she could never expect any place of honour in his life. Chandramukhi, nonetheless, could create space for herself through her selfless service to Debdas and it is quite self-evident when Debdas, towards the end, the night before his death, remembered his mother and remembered another face glowing with utmost purity and affection: the face of Chandramukhi.[64] The juxtaposition of the mother and the fallen woman in his last, unblemished moment had raised Chandramukhi to that pedestal of mainstream ideal of womanhood—purity—which life had so persistently denied her. For this author, as perhaps for his audience, Chandramukhi stood redeemed! She did so by personifying that virtue categorized by society as 'feminine'—the virtue of total sacrifice, including the self. Sacrifice is tantamount to a penance, a denial, a repudiation of her past as a prostitute, the inverse of the ideal womanhood. 'In theory and in practice, both the "good" domestic woman and the "bad" public seductress could attain virtue through loyalty to a man. . . . A courtesan is "chaste" by virtue of her pure intention and moral tenacity.'[65] If there was a normative equation of a woman's moral purity with her sexual chastity, Chandramukhi's character broke that equation; in moving from the margin of society to centre stage, she was quietly diluting both the categories. This was perhaps the woman's response to the creation of those dichotomous categories by men, even though Chandramukhi was herself a man's creation. Her 'feminine' dilution of categories yet does not threaten the structure! The space that it allowed the fallen woman was through the pursuit of 'true' love, counterposed to mere base sexual pleasure, and unmitigated sacrifice, even when this love and sacrifice were not reciprocated. This was the only way she could achieve some status, some space, physical, social or moral.

A similar situation faced Kshiroda in 'Bicharak'.[66] Kshiroda appears before us as a woman past her youth, yet forced by the circumstances to follow, in spite of her utter abhorrence of it, the profession of prostitution for sheer survival. Tagore has indeed highlighted what he perceives as the ugliness, the sordidness of the lives of these unfortunate women, abandoned by society for a little lapse on their part. But then the men, like our hero Mohit

Mohan, stood outside the limits of social morality which bounded the women. Mohit Mohan here is a striking example of a duality of social norms.

> Young girls and widows sometimes yield their honour to their lovers' importunities, and leave their homes and loving relatives with the men whom they adore. It is too late when they awake from the spell that lures them to destruction. The society, it is true, condemns such conduct on the part of the man, but readily forgives him, while it is different with a woman. She has no place in society. Thus the offender escapes, the victim is punished. . . .[67]

Kshiroda in 'Bicharak' out of utter desperation (being cheated by her latest paramour), tried to commit suicide along with her infant son. She jumped into a well to put an end to her miserable existence. But unfortunate as she was, she was saved by the people nearby, and was accused of the murder of her own son. The judge before whom she was produced was the very individual responsible for enticing her out of her parental home and later abandoning her to her fate. The only way he could cover up his guilt, and even could convince himself of his innocence regarding his perfidy was by inverting the responsibility and blaming it on the stereotypical fickleness of womankind especially where it involved their own sexuality. This lent an unassailable self-righteousness to his severest denunciation of the crime committed by such a woman. Kshiroda was consequently sentenced to death.

> The judge was convinced that a woman like her did not deserve any kindness or consideration. The logic behind this attitude was not something unfamiliar. On the one hand the judge could equate Hindu women with the goddess Durga, and on the other he had a deep distrust of women in general. He was convinced that by nature women were wayward and always conspiring to defy social and familial authority. Once you let go of your control over them, there will not be a single chaste woman left in society.[68]

Mohit Mohan was a changed person now. He was acutely orthodox, following all the dictates of superstitious Hindu society. The women of his family were to lead a secluded life, untouched by anything outside the four walls of their *zenana.*

'But once he had done injustice to more than one woman, as a result he now punished women most severely for any moral lapses on their part.'[69]

In the final denouement of the story, Mohit Mohan discovered that the ugly, despicable prostitute was none other than the selfsame innocent, trusting young girl who was seduced and then deserted by him twenty-four years ago. He was all the more chastened by the fact that she had all these years cherished his gift of a ring with his portrait on it as her most precious possession. 'Mohit Mohan looked at the ring, and when he raised his eyes, that sinful disgraced woman before him appeared to be glowing like a resplendent image of a goddess.'[70]

This 'lowly' woman secured a moral space once again by reverting to the mould defined by society, to the *sati-savitri* model.

By allowing moral space to a prostitute, a man does not deem himself accountable to society. It does not constitute transgression or deviance on his part as it would always remain in the nebulous zone of individual realization. Mohit Mohan could visualize the image of a goddess in Kshiroda's time- ravaged face since it did not involve any social risk. Kshiroda's destiny would not have allowed her any leeway to rise even an inch above the predetermined status of a social outcast. The question of sexual chastity, which was of prime significance, pre-empted any alternative. Social or physical spaces, the fact of their constant overlap notwithstanding, were something altogether different in their dimensions relative to moral space. To be allowed to occupy social or physical space even on the margins of mainstream society, a woman had to follow some social norms, some codes of conduct. Savitri in *Charitraheen* is a character who could rise above her 'lowly' status of a 'fallen' woman, and acquire space, both physical and social, within mainstream society as a 'sister' and a selfless soul dedicating her whole existence to doing 'good' to others. The social perception of such a woman was that of a person who could reside on the border with a clearly defined role which excluded her from the status of a wife or a mother. This was a position that denied her any sexual as well as gender role and induced her to practise detachment. Upendra's last advice to Savitri reinforced this notion of self-abnegation: 'The bonds of affection and attachments are no longer for you, Savitri. Once your fate has thrown you out of the confines of society, don't ever try to come back inside it. Rather, try to be useful to society keeping yourself outside its boundaries.'[71]

But, to secure this existence, Savitri had to prove, or the author had to give evidence as to the state of her sexual chastity again and again, establishing its verity beyond any doubt. Evidence coming even from the man who was instrumental in dragging Savitri into this precarious situation.[72] Kshiroda's purity of soul helped her achieve moral space, but it could not guarantee her social space, whereas Savitri's purity of soul had to be combined with her physical purity to secure some sort of a social space, along with physical space as Upendra's 'sister'. Upendra once refused to spend a single night under the same roof with her, after he chanced to discover Savitri at Satish's house. His change of heart arose when he was convinced how full of piety Savitri was, and how she had kept her *satitva* intact through the perilous journey of her life. Society's preoccupation with her 'untouched', 'unharmed' purity of body underlined its anxiety to negate the threat of sexuality emanating from a fallen woman. The woman might have fallen from social rank owing to some unwitting decision taken by her; she might have been disowned by society for no faults of her's; but that should not give her the choice of leading a free life, free from social obligations.[73] She should, in her seclusion, lead an irreproachable, blameless life without disrupting social morality in any way.

Savitri's self-perception, evidently conditioned by male society's perception, was no different. When a desperate Satish proposed marriage to her, she refused. She was a widow, rejected by society as a fallen woman, no good could come out of such a marriage. As for her body, although unharmed, it could not have been offered to a man like Satish.[74]

Unlike Savitri, Rajlakshmi in *Shrikanta* could extend her power quite successfully in different spheres and directions in her diverse incarnations as Piarybaiji, a reputed courtesan, as Shrikanta's beloved Rajlakshmi, as a surrogate mother to her stepchildren and as an affluent householder. As a courtesan, she had a strong hold over her clients, and we are left in no doubt about it even at the initial stage of Shrikanta's encounter with Piary.[75] When Piary transformed herself into Rajlakshmi once again, she could secure a permanent place in Shrikanta's life. Yet, Shrikanta on his part could not think of granting her a socially accepted legal status, nor could Rajlakshmi expect it of him. Not only Shrikanta but other people around her, her stepchildren, her servants and followers, her tenants and the subjects in her *zamindari*, accepted her as quite an important social entity. Rajlakshmi did not have to resort to other people's largesse for physical or social space. Her stable financial condition aided by a bit of innocent subterfuges here and there secured it for her. She often led the people around her assume that Shrikanta and she were a married couple. Not that she did not go back to her Piarybaiji-identity once or twice during their long association, but she invariably reverted to her *sati-savitri* image. Her reward, it seems, was the assurance from Shrikanta that all his life he would remain unmarried and true to her. Marriage with her was absolutely out of the question; he could not overlook his social prestige—his *sambhram*.[76] He of course never felt hesitant in accepting money from Rajlakshmi or leading a plush life at her expense. Shrikanta was not unaware of the reality that the affluence they were living in resulted from Piarybaiji's professional status. Except for making some hollow noises once, Shrikanta never appeared to have shown any reluctance to accept this 'tainted' money. Shrikanta very easily assented to the pretence (of leading a life of conjugality with utmost ease) away from his home and when he could submerge his identity in that of Rajlakshmi. When it was the other way around, when Rajlakshmi proposed to accompany him to Prayag, the city symbolizing holiness and therefore propriety, Shrikanta was crestfallen. The hesitation on his part, even when subsequently rectified, brought home to Rajlakshmi the duality of her status in the eyes of Shrikanta and of society; it also brought home to her the realization that Shrikanta too was living a dual existence: not totally averse to accepting her largesse but unwilling to compromise his honour.

The portrayal of women in a range of characters and roles in our sources would itself negate a uniform image of the subjugated, resourceless, helpless stereotype. Indeed, her femininity, even her sexuality itself is turned into a resource deployed to create and enlarge space and carve out an individual from a stereotype. It is to a more detailed examination of individuality that we turn in the following chapter.

NOTES AND REFERENCES

1. Vanaja Dhruvarajan, *Hindu Women and the Power of Ideology*, New Delhi: Vistaar Publication, 1989, p. 40.
2. David Beetham, *The Legitimation of Power*, London: Macmillan Education Ltd., 1991, p. 107.
3. Lyle Kohler, *A Search for Power. 'The Weaker Sex' in Seventeenth Century New England*, Urbana, Chicago, London: University of Illinois Press, 1980, p. 181.
4. Bankim Chatterjee, *Bishabriksha.*
5. F.A. Steel, *Text for India*, London, 1902, p. 157, as in Janaki Nair, 'Uncovering the Zenana: Vision of Indian Womanhood in English Women's Writings, 1830-1940', in Cheryl Johnson-Odin and Margaret Strobel, eds., *Expanding the Boundaries of Woman's History*, Indianapolis, 1992.
6. Ibid., pp. 245-6.
7. Humayun Kabir, *The Bengali Novel*, Calcutta: Firma K.L. Mukhopadhyay, 1968, p. 15.
8. Bankim Chatterjee, *Debichoudhurani*, pp. 646, 657 and *passim.*
9. Ibid., p. 669. In Bengali ritual order, a married woman is required to consume fish on the eleventh day of the moon. Shreekumar Banerjee found in the adherence to this tradition Prafulla's 'unbounded love' for her husband; see his *Banga Sahitye Upanyaser Dhara*, Calcutta: Modern Book Agency, 1984, p. 93. Our perception is slightly different here, for we prefer to look at it as socialization.
10. Ibid., p. 717. Tanika Sarkar has interpreted this action of *Debi* who 'lays down the glorious garb of the robber queen and turns to dish-washing' as the symbol of patriarchy's manoeuvring skill and power relation to ensure that 'the woman has a specific and limited role and there is no final and absolute transgression'. Tanika Sarkar, 'Nationalist Iconography: Image of Women in 19th Century Bengali Literature', *EPW*, 21 Nov. 1987, p. 2011.
11. Ibid., p. 543.
12. Arvind Sharma, 'Notes and Communication: The Gita, Suttee and Rammohun Roy', *The Indian Economic and Social History Review*, 20, 3, 1983, pp. 382-3.

13. Dorothy Ko, *Teachers of the Inner Chamber: Women and Culture in 17th Century China*, Stanford: Stanford University Press, 1994, p. 89.
14. *Gribadaba*, p. 538.
15. Simone de Beauvoir, *The Second Sex*, Eng. tr. H.M. Parshley, London: Picador, 1988, p. 666.
16. Sarat Chatterjee, *Datta*, pp. 365-6.
17. Sarat Chatterjee, *Charitraheen*, p. 136.
18. Ibid., pp. 182-3.
19. Ibid., p. 183.
20. Ibid. p. 233.
21. For the concept of role, see Michael Banton, *Roles: An Introduction to the Study of Social Relations*, London: Tavistock Publications, 1965; Robert K. Merton, *Social Theory and Social Structure*, enlarged edn., New York: Free Press, 1968; Erving Goffman, *The Representation of Self in Everyday Life*, New York: Doubleday Anchor Books, 1959.
22. Tagore, 'Streer Patra' (short story), *Rabindra Rachnavali*, vol. 7, Tagore Centenary edn., Calcutta: Govt. of West Bengal, 1961.
23. Tagore, 'Poila Number' (short story), ibid.
24. Tagore, 'Streer Patra', p. 638.
25. Ibid., p. 647
26. Ibid.
27. Sarat Chatterjee, *Debdas*, p. 65.
28. Tagore, 'Manbhanjan' (short story).
29. Vanaja Dhruvarajan, *Hindu Women and the Power of Ideology*, p. 40.
30. Tagore, 'Manbhanjan', p. 289.
31. Sarat Chatterjee, *Sheshprashna*, p. 225.
32. Ibid., p. 230
33. Leela Dube, 'On the Construction of Gender', in Karuna Chanana, ed., *Socialization, Education and Women*, p. 181.
34. Shirley Ardener, 'Ground Rules and Social Maps for Women: An Introduction', in S. Ardener, ed., *Women and Space: Ground Rules and Social Maps*, London: Croom Helm, 1981, p. 19.
35. Doranne Jacobson observes: 'Women also help make important decisions in other family matters (especially in the selection of mates for their children). Men do some of the scouting, but, through their networks of ties with women in other towns and villages, women frequently have access to information vital for evaluating prospects.' See her 'The Women of North and Central India: Goddesses and Wives', in D. Jacobson and Susan S. Wadley, *Women in India: Two Perspectives*, New Delhi: Manohar, 1977, p. 63.
36. V. Dhruvarajan, *Hindu Women and the Power of Ideology*, p. 40.
37. Sarat Chatterjee, *Parineeta*, p. 109. Somewhat of an echo of this one encounters in Mernissi, Fatima, commenting upon the role of a mother in Moroccan society, 'According to my interview with traditional

women, it is the mother, not the son, who initiates the marriage, makes the decision about the creation of her son's new family, although officially this is supposed to be the role of the son's father'. And this she observes, '*significantly reduces the man's decision making role*' (emphasis added), Mernissi, *Beyond the Veil: Male Female Dynamics in Muslim Society*, revd. edn., London: Al Saqi Books, 1985.

38. Sudhir Kakar, *The Inner World: A Psycho-analytic Study of Childhood and Society in India*, 2nd edn., New Delhi: OUP, 1992, p. 118. Dorothy Ko in her *Teachers of the Inner Chamber* has also reflected upon this 'discrepancy' between 'what should be' and 'what is' as a key to understanding the 'Janus-faced nature' of the seventeenth-century Chinese society, p. 9.
39. Bankim Chatterjee, *Debichoudhurani*, p. 714.
40. David Beetham, *The Legitimation of Power*, pp. 78-9.
41. Ibid., p. 80.
42. Meenakshi Mukherjee, 'Story, History and Her Story', *Studies in History*, 9, 1, 1993, p. 76.
43. *Debichoudhurani*, p. 717.
44. Ibid., p. 716.
45. Tagore, 'Streer Patra', p. 638.
46. Ibid., p. 648.
47. 'Feminine India wisely does not discard femininity when she takes to affairs and politics', Pamela Henkson, *Indian Harvest*, London: Collins, 1941, p. 73.
48. Title of section heading in Christian Klapisch-Zuber's editorial note, *Silences of the Middle Ages*, vol. II of Georges Duby and Michelle Perrot, general eds., *A History of Women in the West*, Belknap, Cambridge, Mass.: Harvard University Press, 1992, p. 161.
49. 'Aparichita', p. 681.
50. Tagore, *Ghare Baire*, p. 438.
51. Michelle Perrot, 'Women, Power and History', in Michelle Perrot, ed., *Writing Women's History*, p. 167.
52. Tagore, *Chokher Bali*, p. 374.
53. Michelle Perrot, 'Women, Power and History', p. 169.
54. Tagore, *Gora*, p. 23.
55. Ibid., p. 13.
56. Ibid., p. 350.
57. Ibid., p. 52.
58. Dorothy Ko, *Teachers of the Inner Chamber*, p. 171.
59. Lynda Nead, *Myths of Sexuality: Representation of Women in Victorian Britain*, Oxford: Basil Blackwell, 1988, p. 95.
60. *Debdas*, p. 44.
61. Ibid.
62. Ibid., p. 71.

63. Ibid.
64. Ibid., p. 74.
65. Dorothy Ko, *Teachers of the Inner Chamber*, p. 257.
66. Tagore, 'Bicharak' (short story).
67. Santosh Kumar Mukherji, *Prostitution in India*, Calcutta: Dasgupta & Co., n.d., pp. 316-17.
68. 'Bicharak', p. 252.
69. Ibid., p. 255.
70. Ibid., pp. 255-6.
71. *Charitraheen*, p. 336.
72. Ibid., p. 309.
73. S.F. Nadel, *The Theory of Social Structure*, London: Cohen and West, 1957, pp. 49-50.
74. *Charitraheen*, pp. 318-19.
75. Sarat Chatterjee, *Shrikanta*, pp. 419, 422.
76. Ibid., p. 529.

CHAPTER 4

Search for Identity

Thus humanity is male and man defines woman not in herself but as relates to him; she is not regarded as an autonomous being. . . .[1]

Such is the world-view that has acquired almost universal hegemony in the feminist discourse. Indeed, this is virtually how feminism defines itself. But then an unqualified acceptance of this world-view would perhaps result in the guilt of ignoring a major episode in the drama enacted perpetually in the relationship between the two sexes. For it overlooks the possibility of the presence and growth of a distinct sense of self-identity amongst women precisely in the ambience of the socially governed restriction of their roles and status, placing these under strict male gaze, authority and dominance. It is in this restrictive context that the women's relentless endeavour to establish their separate identity and assert their individuality becomes all the more arresting. To achieve this, to carve out their identity, women often traversed onto the path of confrontation. Confrontation is not an attribute that is conventionally associated with a woman; hence its enhanced significance in the present context. Added to it was the question of unequal power distribution and opportunities available to women in the patriarchal social setting. As a result the expression of women's individuality has often been characterized by a persistent questioning mixed with a bit of resentment inherent against, if not outright opposition to, male authority and dominance and these aspects eventually had crystallized into non-conformity with accepted social norms as the symbol of women's growing individuality. One would discern very clear expression of this trait in many of the women we are presently dealing with.

It is striking that all these women, with the singular exception of Anandamayee in *Gora*, were denied motherhood by the authors. This denial itself imparts to them a certain uniqueness of identity, for conformity to the stereotype would imply a woman's ultimate fulfilment in fecundity. Besides, the characters on their part question the legitimacy of even the concept of wifehood—that very enveloping status which was to be their very raison d'être. Interestingly it is not the women themselves who sought to shrug off the responsibility of motherhood. Indeed, they valued the experience of motherhood as the very expression of their femininity, as the expression of their freedom. Sudhir Kakar in his *The Inner World* has very emphatically underlined the significance of motherhood in a woman's life.

> For an Indian woman, imminent motherhood is not only the personal fulfilment of an old wish and biological consummation of a life-long promise, but an event in which the culture confirms her status as a renewer of the race, and extends to her a respect and consideration which were not accorded to her as a mere wife. It is not surprising that this improvement in her social relations and status within the family, the resolution of her emotional conflicts and discovery of a way of organizing her future life around the core of motherliness tend to be experienced unconsciously as a gift from the child growing within her. The unborn child is perceived as her saviour. . . . In the case of a Hindu woman, at least in the imagery of the culture, maternal feelings of tenderness and nurturance occur in combination with a profound gratitude and the readiness for a poignantly high emotional investment in the child.[2]

Mrinal in 'Streer Patra', perhaps the most individualistic of all women characters in this study, expressed the anguish of the missed motherhood without a trace of ambiguity. She envisioned motherhood which eluded her, as an experience which could uplift women from the daily drudgery, cruelty and meanness that surrounded ordinary middle class women's existence.

My daughter died immediately after her birth. I too, was at the threshold of death as if she beckoned me to accompany her. If alive, she could have imparted all that is truly noble and sublime to my existence. Motherhood would have been much more ennobling than my status as the second daughter-in-law of your family. Motherhood gives one that sense of freedom which transports a woman from the narrow confines of her life to the universality of her experience. I only suffered the agony and the pain of motherhood, but was denied the freedom that comes with it.[3]

But this was motherhood born of choice rather than of social diktat; hence the association of freedom with it, which Tagore realized in a fleeting moment. But the almost universal denial of motherhood to the women characters by the male authors was, on one hand, a recognition of the socially ordained stereotype and on the other a unique defiance of it, as a way of lifting these characters out of straitjackets. In the author's perception, for a mother, her child's interest or welfare assumes primacy, her sense of the self automatically gets relegated to secondary position or at least temporarily shelved. This is demonstrated in the case of Kumudini in *Jogajog*. Kumudini much against her earlier resolution decided to go back to her husband's home as she realized that she could not have deprived her unborn child of its rightful parentage. It is thus that the authors created a dichotomy between motherhood and individuality and in order to impart the latter to their characters denied them the former.

If we selected three characters from Sarat; Abhaya, Kiranmayee and Kamal[4] as unconventional or non-conformist we will notice how their unconventionality often merged with stereotyped image of a traditional woman—thus dissolving the supposed dichotomy between the two poles—traditionality or conformity and individuality.

Both Kiranmayee and Abhaya were in a way social rebels, for their life was lived as an explicit statement against their society and community. They were not *patibratas* in the conventional sense of the term, although at one or the other point of their life, they tried to emulate the idea quite fervently. But circumstances, at least in the case of Abhaya, were so adverse that she had to acknowledge the futility of her endeavour and refused to succumb to the social diktat that for her would mean surrendering to the most ignominious of all experiences. This fleeting brush with convention brings into focus her strong unconventionality. Abhaya was prepared even to share her husband, knowing him to be a perfect rogue, with his Burmese wife and children. But her inner strength, her confidence in her own self, such as were manifest throughout in small little things in her life, received a severe beating at the hands of her husband. He not only did not show her the respect a wife would expect from her husband, but doubted her integrity and her chastity.

> I had to come back to the man who once married me, but that did not solve my problem. His second wife, his children, his love—I have no claim over any of these; yet do I have to live with him and find my life's fulfilment in that existence prostituting my self-respect and sense of dignity?[5]

Along with this Abhaya raised a basic question—the question of the ordained duality of values in society.[6] If marriage vows were something sacrosanct for women, so should they be for men. 'When I lost my wifely status and even the privilege of motherhood, why should I be tied down to a man who is not only cruel and dishonest, a debauch too and sacrifice everything that I want to be or to do?'[7]

She was quite unequivocal in her assertion that she was not going to stick to an unworthy husband and in the process be oblivious of the selfless love and affection of another man who sacrificed his normal life amongst his friends and relations for her sake. It was not a very easy decision to take. To cast off the stranglehold of traditional social norms and to accept someone who would be socially recognized as a *parpurush*—the other man, someone else other than her husband—required an enormous amount of strength of character and determination. Abhaya could take that decision and resolved to make a meaningful beginning out of their dismal existence in an unfamiliar locale. The unfamiliar surroundings are clearly a metaphor for the setting up of a new life, unbounded by the familiar social inhibitions; here Abhaya could truly seek out a new identity. In the process, she managed to put forward quite a few cogent questions about the validity of the concept of a devoted wife, in life and in death; her search for self-identity in its essence sought out an equality of relationship between man and woman—in marriage or outside it where the sanctioned relationship had been heavily weighted in favour of men.

Individuality, or self-articulation for that matter, has never been an attribute readily and favourably recognized in women.

> Individuality does not command, and never has commanded such respect in India as it does in the West. Self suppression, not self expression or self development, is still, as it has always been, the highest ideal of the best Indian minds. Individual initiatives in which the Western world puts its trust, is in India restrained by a multitude of inhibitions.[8]

Contrary to the impression conveyed here, Kiranmayee in *Charitraheen*, had these qualities in abundance. It is not very easy to categorize her character and to cast her in a predictable stereotypical mould. The element of unpredictability in her nature made her quite a complex character and this complexity was the accumulated upshot of her acute sense of deprivation—physical, emotional, sexual and psychological. She had been, she felt, cheated out of all the good things of life. With all her flawless beauty, razor sharp intelligence and a discriminating mind, she was nevertheless married to a man who could, perhaps, never assuage her natural urge for leading a normal married life.[9] She was not entirely an ignorant person, a woman accepting her fate and the inherent injustice involved in it without a murmur. She never tried to establish her credentials as a devoted and loyal wife either in public or in private and challenged the concept of undying devotion to one's husband by stating categorically that she never loved her husband.[10] The question of sexual fidelity also, she believed, was not something to be treated absolutely objectively or in isolation. Sexuality, in her perception, was something natural and normal in a human being and she did not intend to keep it under wraps forever. She admitted to her sexual dalliance with the family doctor not so much with a sense of guilt as with a feeling of revulsion. If she divested sexuality of its social inhibitions, her detour into an extramarital fling was not completely without remorse. But far more than the actual sexual experience with the doctor, it is the open admission of it which signified her departure from the norm and assertion of her self.

'Do you know of such a thirst which drive a man even to the thick polluted sewage water? I had that compulsion, that urge; for long I had kept it locked inside me, and then it came out and came out in this form.' If this one detour was not enough to mark her out as a person, her candid affirmation of her true feelings for Upendra reinforced that identity. At that precise moment when she was trying to come to terms with her life, its barrenness and ugliness, with all her emotional yearnings unfulfilled, there appeared in her life the 'ideal' man, the 'ideal' husband Upendra. The emotional turmoil, the tension that arose out of her interaction with Upendra was quite overwhelming. The floodgates of her pent up passions and emotions opened up and engulfed her whole being. In Upendra she could find the apostle of her unfulfilled love and unconventional as she was she did not deem it necessary to hide her feelings from Upendra or to keep them locked up in her heart as a secret. She established her distinctive identity by insisting that Upendra should know about her emotions first and then decide about his future course of action regarding Kiranmayee's fate. If she, after her husband's death, had to depend upon and live on the munificence of Upendra and his wife Surobala, the burden of her indebtedness would be somewhat lighter if only he could acknowledge and appreciate her sentiment, even without reciprocating it. She could find her identity in the fact that Upendra's generosity was not absolutely a nameless, faceless gesture without any personal involvement. Significantly, even here the initiative is taken by the woman who had the confidence of surviving a rejection. If self-articulation and attempt 'to act on their own judgement and initiative'[11] on the part of women, are considered a definite manifestation of women's heightened sense of self and growing individuality, one does not fail to recognize a singular identity in Kiranmayee's character.

If Kiranmayee resented the cruelty of an unjust and unequal marital relationship, Kamal questioned the institution of marriage itself. Freedom from all ritualistic and customary bondages, according to her, was the essence of true relationship between a man and a woman. 'Marriage like other things in life is just an incidental happening. The true tragedy in women's life started from the day when we decided to consider it the ultimate aim in a woman's life.'[12] Kamal's utterances did not mark a mere inversion of the existing structure of relationship; they went far beyond in that they liberated men as much as the women; they constituted an alternative *weltanschauung* altogether. About her own mother, Kamal's comments were equally startling: 'She was beautiful no doubt, but she did not have good taste. I was born three years after my father's death.'[13] As a matter of fact the unconventionality is integral to her identity—in her unconventional parentage—her mother a Bengali and her 'father' an English tea planter and she was not a strictly legitimate offspring, although she spent the first nineteen years of her life with this English father of hers. Her unorthodox statement about another woman's life once more bears testimony to her individuality. Against the effusive mediocrity of Harendra's praise for Neelima (widowed sister-in-law of Abinash) as a divine picture of self-sacrifice, of ideal womanhood and widowhood, Kamal's brutally cutting comment on the futility of such an existence stands out in sharp relief.

> Being the mistress of someone else's household and the mother of someone else's motherless children might be the highest example of self-abnegation, but how do you know it is the right thing to do? People might have glorified the selfless role in the highest terms but it is after all playacting—doing something by proxy, there is no honour in it.[14]

Of these three characters Kamal is most loudly assertive of her individuality, her identity. We find her tirelessly defying all the social norms and codes of normative behaviour. She was fiercely protective of her own freedom of action and word. But at one point all three characters submerge their individual identity in the feminine role model. Abhaya on her part always aspired to fulfil herself as a wife and a mother. Kiranmayee's frustration was the culmination of her annoyance at the denial of her feminine aspirations. Consequently the expressions of their femininity were quite in keeping with their basic nature. The most surprising instance here; however, is Kamal in *Sheshprashna*. Her character is not linear; with all her emancipation, bold assertion and the confidence to shock by questioning all that is sacrosanct, Kamal still subscribed to the socially accepted image of womanhood ascribed to the women's subconscious psyche to act the mother figure to the demanding yet helpless male—the fan-wielding woman serving food with utmost care to her man. This ambivalence ingrained in her character also prompted her to become a vegetarian after her first husband's death[15] and this coming from a woman who defended so forcefully the individual freedom of choice—to remain outside marriage ties and to live-in with a man not her husband. Even after her much vaunted assertion of her self-identity 'Kamal is not anyone's property—she is the master of herself',[16] she followed Ajit to Amritsar to lead a parasitical existence. Male protection assumes an importance that envelops them all.

Mrinal in 'Streer Patra' on the other hand was an individual without being self-conscious about it. It was an individuality she was born with; it lay in her action, not in verbal assertion. And this inner strength of character, which she had carried within herself more or less silently, gave her the confidence to write to her husband 'To you I am only the second daughter-in-law of the family. After all these years, standing face to face with the vast expanse of the sea, I realized I do have another identity, another relationship with this wide world, with my god. This is not a letter from your *mejobou*—the second daughter in law.'[17] Again 'I am not going back to your house at Makhan Baral Lane. Bindu had helped me realize my worth, my value there. I do not want to go into it any more.'[18] 'One's full name; whatever one is thereafter called, loss of one's name can be a great curtailment of the self.'[19] What Goffman has termed a 'great curtailment of the self' in an entirely different context carries meaning in the instance of Mrinal's assertion that she would never go back to her marital home as only their *mejobou*, and ends her final letter to her husband with her first name Mrinal, thereby asserting her sense of self, of her individual identity.

Mrinal's final decision leaves a question mark in the mind of the reader. One feels curious to know what actually Mrinal did with her life after leaving her husband's house for good. But clearly the storyteller would leave that open ended. To give her a 'happy' life thereafter would be like a fairy tale ending; to depict her life as miserable would reinforce the stereotype. At any rate, it was her individual freedom that was at stake, not her material well-being. For, her decision was characterized by a total rejection of male hegemony and patriarchal authority. When she concluded her letter with a telling metaphor of turning away from the 'protective feet' of her husband—'*Tomader Caranatalasrayacchinna Mrinal*'—she was rejecting both the trampling of her individuality as well as the quotidian protection the feet had provided.

Indeed with the passage of time, from Bankim to Tagore, we find women going from strength to strength—a definite shaping up of their individuality, their identity, carving out a niche in the society where they were always expected to play the secondary roles.[20] In Bankim's *Bishabriksha* everything revolved round Nagendra, the hero. Kundanandini was a passive recipient of his attention, whereas in Tagore's *Chokher Bali* Binodini herself took the initiative of diverting the hero's attention from his wife towards herself. Kunda in her childlike innocence and trust in Nagendra was prepared to end her life when she discovered that she was in the eye of a controversy and it was she whose life and love were superfluous in the existing scheme of things. Binodini did not find death as the ultimate solution to the situation created by her actions—she decided to withdraw, to detach herself and did it with much dignity, without sacrificing her self-esteem and did it on her own terms. Kunda had been projected as a helpless victim of her destiny whereas Binodini was in full control over it. Whatever she was doing was done with a very clear perception of the consequences. Suryamukhi of the same novel *Bishabriksha* did leave home as Mrinal did in 'Streer Patra', but there ended the similarity between these two characters, Suryamukhi left home not so much as a protest against her husband's indifference towards her (as he took a second wife) but out of her frustration, her desperation in her knowledge that she could no longer hold her husband's attention, could no longer play the pivotal role in his life as she used to do. Without her husband's love and care, her whole world turned out to be a complete void. Again, she wanted to come back home to have a last look at her husband; after that death would be a welcome escape. Mrinal's decision to leave home, on the other hand, presents an entirely different world-view. Mrinal left home not because she found anything particularly lacking in her husband or his household. She left it to discover herself, to find an existence which perhaps would not be approved of by society but which would give her a sense of freedom. And for her, that was much more valuable than her life as a wife or a daughter-in-law, which gave her routine respectability but deprived her of the realization of her conviction, of her new found belief and above all her entity as an individual. In her life her husband and her home became irrelevant. Women, she discovered, could seek out and find an alternative existence where she would not have to die a thousand deaths, everyday, every moment of her life, the existence which might be devoid of all comforts that cushioned her life, but which would give her a rare strength, impart a rare sense of confidence in her own worth and sense of dignity. But self-identity is something which perhaps could not be achieved in absolute, total void. 'Virtually all the occasions for talking or writing about the self involved a relationship: with God or God and one's confessor, with a patron, with a friend or a lover, or specially with one's family and lineage.'[21] Severing all her relationship with her familiar space, her milieu, Mrinal established a new relationship with her God that was manifest not in the images or the idols in the temples, but in the elements of nature 'the vast blue expanse of the ocean before me and the dark mass of monsoon clouds over head'[22] and she emulated legendary Meerabai. Meera left everything behind in search of God and stuck to her conviction in spite of the heavy burden of restrictions and opposition and Mrinal too was going to seek out the meaning of her existence by doing so.

The pursuit of the emerging individuality and self-identity of women stops short as if in front of a closed door when one encounters Haimanti—the heroine of the story of the same name.[23] Why did Haimanti put up with the indignity heaped upon her and all the more on her father by her in-laws? Why could she not break away from it all and go back to her father's where she would have been welcome any time? One feels tempted to draw a parallel between her character and the character of her counterpart in Tagore's 'Aparichita'. One finds the same innocence, same uprightness and love of truth in both the characters. Kalyani in 'Aparichita' chose to remain single and lead an independent life after her disastrous experience on her wedding day. She has been termed as the first heroine of Tagore to be 'absolutely self-reliant'.[24] The historian B.B. Majumdar has preferred to call her one of emerging new types of heroines in Tagore's literature.[25] Haimanti on the other hand chose to remain with her husband at her in-laws' home and ultimately accept death. Was it because of the quality of conjugal love and relationship she shared with her husband who himself was a 'victim' of the social construction which prompted him to prove himself a good son first, before being a good husband? The lurking image of our eternal model hero Ramachandra is easily discernible here. Haimanti could realize how helpless her young husband was in the face of the combined force of traditional social and familial pressure and that, perhaps, decided the issue in his favour.[26] She did not want to deprive him of her companionship which must have been a much needed source of comfort and solace to him.

Usha Nilsson in her 'Women in contemporary Indian literature' has observed a strong sense of self-identity, a sense of parity with men, etc., '. . . without being aggressive or apologetic about it' as characteristics of a 'new woman'.[27] While an unhappy dichotomy between an archetypal 'old woman' and the emerging 'new woman' is embedded in the very construction of either of these stereotypes, the attributes of the 'new woman' are noticeable in plenty in the genre of young women we are dealing with. Bharati in Sarat's *Patherdabi* is one such character, with adequate amount of education and enlightenment, with an unorthodox background, Bharati, in spite of her widely different upbringing fell in love with Apurba. She was a Christian living in the house of her mother's second husband and Apurba hailed from a rather orthodox Brahmin family and was ever so conscious and careful of his status in society. Bharati naturally was not very sure about the future of this relationship. Nonetheless, she never tried to deny her feelings towards him. Her love for Apurba was quite transparent. At the same time she had complete trust in her worth as an individual. She believed that she could lead an independent and purposeful existence even without Apurba. 'My love for Apurba is genuine, no doubt, I have loved him with all the good and the bad things in his character and I will never be able to banish him from my life or my mind. But that does not mean that if I cannot spend the rest of my life as his wife, I will be left with an existence entirely meaningless and futile. No, it is not true at all.'[28] This confident note and the quiet realization of life's intrinsic worth were part of women's growing strength that arose out of the expanding horizon opening up before them.

Lalita in *Gora* could very easily be considered one of these 'new women'. As soon as she is introduced in the novel her distinct sense of self-identity appears to be apparent and self-evident. 'She is not much of a talker, and follows her own rules and laws. She is quite capable of speaking her mind out whenever necessary. Even her mother is slightly scared of her and thinks twice before interfering in her affairs.'[29] In Sucharita and Lalita, in their respective search for identity, one finds certain difference in attitudes towards what they wanted to accomplish and what they actually managed to achieve. In Sucharita, the sense of identity tended to get diluted, not so much because of the absence of any clear perspective about what she wanted to do but because she was more worried about what others expected her to do. Lalita, on the other hand, felt not least bit restricted while following the dictates of her conscience. For her, thinking out something and acting accordingly happened automatically and ever so naturally. After much persuasion she finally agreed to go with her mother and sisters to a suburban town where the wife of the local British Official was organizing a cultural fare. The young people had gathered there to participate. But things took a precipitous turn when Lalita came to know about the humiliation Gora had to suffer at the hand of the English officer and his subsequent imprisonment. While Sucharita chose to suffer in silence than to go against Lalita's mother's express wishes, it did not take Lalita a moment to decide her future plan of action. She felt so outraged at the idea of being a party to the cultural bonanza under the patronage of the same British officer that she decided to leave the place immediately much against the earnest protestations of her mother. She eventually accompanied Benoy, without his prior knowledge, on her way back to Calcutta. This simple act of defiance of societal norms demonstrated an enormous amount of self-confidence and this was the quality which endeared her to her upright and truthful father. Paresh Babu could discover in his daughter's character the presence of a rare strength and distinct individuality.[30] She exhibited the same distinctiveness expressed in self-articulation when she declared in the presence of her parents that she could not see anything wrong in the possibility of her marriage with Benoy even if he had not embraced Brahmoism. And the most important thing which she learnt from her father was that she should be able to use her own judgement and that was how she was going to vindicate her assumption.

Sucharita, on the other hand never acted in haste, in an impulsive manner. Her endeavour had always been to conform to the accepted pattern of behaviour and as far as possible not to create any inconvenience or to cause heartbreak and anguish to her foster parents. Here we could find the key to their divergent behaviour; one with natural parents and the other being brought up by foster parents, and all the time being reminded of her duty and responsibility towards them, at least by her foster mother.

While discussing the question of individuality in a woman (or a man) and her self-identity, we often tend to treat this as an attribute of modern Western society. A teleology is established between the emergence of the individual and the industrial economy and its concomitant culture. Thus Meenakshi Mukherjee observes 'the growth of individualism in English fiction after the eighteenth century can be related among other factors, to the new social mobility that industrialization had made possible making man realize his unique potential outside a rigid hierarchy . . .'. But Mukherjee does not see any corresponding movement on the Indian scene.[31] Therefore the assertion that the 'new woman' with self-identity, was the product of 'economic freedom resulting from education and job opportunities'[32] among other things becomes a cause for some discomfort for us. The teleology implicated here between industrial economy and the valorization of one's identity as the universally valid construct appears to be somewhat of a reductionist argument in which individuality is solely predicated upon economic independence and education, etc. Indeed this is a construction of individuality by the urban educated middle class in it own image, which amounts to a denial of it to the rural women, to the housewife, to the mother and so forth, for devoid of the pre-conditions they cannot possibly possess and certainly cannot articulate, their personal identity.

Bankim has often been accused of conventionality, his women always subscribing to the preordained script, abiding by the ascriptive norms of behaviour. The search for identity conventionally starts with Mrinal in 'Streer Patra' and Anila in 'Poila Number', but does not necessarily end there. Suryamukhi in *Bishabriksha* said 'who am I? Your happiness is mine, if you marry Kunda, I will be happy.' No greater proof of a woman's complete denial of self-identity is considered necessary. But when the same woman raised the question 'Kamal, do you know of a place where girls are killed as soon as they are born?'[33] The resentment inherent in it is manifest—resentment against the socially conceived ideal of womanhood dictating them to suffer silently having sacrificed their happiness for the sake of their men. To Suryamukhi death was preferable to such an existence where one had to surrender completely to the norms laid down by society, and perhaps ungrudgingly. On the other hand, Debi, in *Debichoudhurani* wanted to come back to the fold as Prafulla, leaving behind her entire estate and establishment of which she was the undisputed master, again in search of her identity which she felt, was to be found in her role as the devoted wife of a loving husband. It might appear to be an outrageous idea to exchange her freedom, her loyal following, her power over a number of people, her role as an individual for the role of a stereotypical housewife, but the author portrays *her* as taking this decision and seeking fulfilment in this role. It is rather difficult to put the question of self-identity in a limited slot and determine preconditions for its expression. The search for identity or some expression of aspirations on the part of Bankim's women, as in the case of Prafulla, was quite clearly manifested. For Prafulla, left alone in the midst of a jungle and without any place to go back to, suicide would have been the easy answer to her precarious existence. But like Indira in the novel of the same name,[34] the question of suicide did not occur to her perhaps owing to some psycho-socio-religious factors which present ample scope for investigation. Whereas Indira would have welcomed death coming in any other way except suicide, Prafulla decided to tackle the whole affair in her own way. She was of course, made of what we call 'sterner stuff' and went about finding a way out of her predicament. She did not break down under the enormous pressure of hostile circumstances, nor did she falter in her search for a somewhat marginal existence thereafter. Obviously, Bankim's women, in spite of being conventional, were not exactly doormats as they are believed to be. They could at least think of their separate existence and identity, even when it caused enormous amounts of emotional upheaval and heart-break, away from their husbands and family protection. Prafulla proved her identity by transforming herself from an illiterate village girl to the legendary Debichoudhurani. Indira's transformation was neither so dramatic nor so spectacular; nonetheless, she took initiatives to mould her future life where she could expect to get back her husband's affection and acceptance in his family. Sagar, in *Debichoudhurani*, exhibited this streak of individuality when she reprimanded her husband spiritedly for pushing her with his toe. Sagar let go of her husband's feet and raised her head like a highly enraged snake, 'did you kick me'? On Brajeshwar's part it was absolutely unintentional and accidental; had he admitted that, it would have been enough. But in his anxiety-ridden exasperated mood, Sagar's accusation was the last straw.

'What if I did so, even your wealthy father worshipped these feet once.' (Brajeshwar has come to his in-laws to borrow money in a bid to save his father's estate but fails to convince his 'wealthy' father-in-law.) 'That was a mistake', Sagar said, 'I am going to atone for it'. When Brajeshwar asked her if she was going to kick him back, Sagar retorted 'no, I can't stoop so low, but if I am the daughter of a real brahmin, then' . . . someone finished her sentence from behind 'you will take my feet on your lap and press them as a servant does' and she repeated it as she was going to say something of that sort on her own.[35]

Prafulla was there behind the scene and her ingenuity saved the situation as she helped Sagar fulfil her vow. The protest in this show of servility was palpable. Even Brajeshwar's mother, always faithfully following her husband's wishes, asserted her identity by reminding Brajeshwar about his duty to a woman, when Brajeshwar's father asked him to throw Prafulla out of his house. 'No Son, don't ever treat a woman in that manner. You will have to carry out your father's order, fine, but don't I have any right to say anything? Whatever you may do, don't ill-treat her.'[36]

All these sparks of individuality that we encounter are demonstrated generally by women who we conveniently stamp as conventional and without any original perspective on life. Their lives are guided by the accepted social norms. These women had never tried much to break out of the stereotypical roles and status prescribed by society. They had rather kept themselves within the limits drawn out for them. Nonetheless, when pushed to the corner they had exhibited some strength and resourcefulness in establishing their identity which all their lives they had learnt to keep under the wraps. In this context perhaps it would not be much of a digression if we cite the example of the heroine of Sarat's *Bamuner Meye.* Sandhya, a moderately educated village girl, obviously had her own set of values, in which getting married at an appropriate age to a tolerably eligible man was on the forefront. Born in a Kulin family, she could never forget her pride and position in the caste hierarchy. Her marriage with Arun, a social outcast (because of his trip to a foreign land and having belonged to a lower rank in Brahminical hierarchy) was out of the question. But when on the day of her marriage, the secret about her father's questionable parenthood was disclosed in public and the bridegroom left unceremoniously, Sandhya did not have anything else but to turn to Arun, with the plea to save her from the 'imminent' social disgrace. Arun, riding over his initial hesitation, expressed his willingness to accept her as his wife. But Sandhya by then had decided about her future plans and did not hesitate to answer back,

> Yes, that day I was rather lost and confused and did not know what I was doing. That phase is over and now I know what I should do. I would like to find out if women can live a life of their own without achieving the 'ultimate' in their life, that is getting married and that is the reason why I am going away from this place along with my father.[37]

The same sentiment, of course in an entirely different context, was expressed again and again by Kamal in *Sheshprashna.* She questioned the legitimacy of the institution of marriage but her point of argument seemed to have been bogged down in the quagmire of sermonizing and philosophizing. The cacophony of arguments was raucous enough to drown the real issue altogether. Sandhya being on the opposite side of the pole (Sandhya had a closed, tradition bound orthodox upbringing whereas Kamal was the illegitimate daughter of an English tea-planter and a Bengali mother—an extremely unconventional parentage) had nothing against marriage as such, what she wanted to do was to look for a life beyond it, an alternative existence.

With a grim determination, quite unexpected in a girl of her station, she proceeded to seek out an identity of her own. Kamal, on the other hand, did not hesitate to welcome a cushioned existence with Ajit without, of course, going through the hassle of socially sanctified bonds of relationship.

Nirupama, in Tagore's 'Dena Paona' is a very commonplace young girl with nothing extraordinary in her character to mark her out as an individual. She was married off at a tender age to a rich family by her doting father and there started the tragedy of her life. Her father failed to meet the demands of dowry of her avaricious in-laws and she, as a consequence, was leading an absolutely miserable life. When her father came to see her in-laws with money which he had at last procured by selling off his ancestral property, she sent him back with unexpected astuteness 'No father, this money, if you pay to my in-laws, would add to the humiliation I am subjected to in this house. Don't I have any other identity? Will I be treated as a money bag only? As long as there is money in it, it will have some value, otherwise not?'[38] This sudden awakening of the sense of her individual identity in spite of her comparative young age and perhaps lack of any formal education helps reinforce our assumption that the sense of the self is not always pre-conditioned; its expression has an extremely variegated ambience as its backdrop constituting both innate psychic resources in human beings as well as the social spaces encompassing their lives. In Nirupama's mental horizon a life away from her husband and in-laws, even at her parent's, was not a very cogent or clearly etched out possibility. The socialization she had been subjected to from her childhood taught her to be tolerant. '*Dharitrir mato Sahansila hao*'—be tolerant like the mother earth. And, tolerant she was. Nirupama did not complain and she had to pay for her defiance with her life at the end. As far as there was some semblance of hope in recovering the promised amount from her father, there was only a lack of interest and indifference to her well-being on the part of her in-laws. When the fact came to light that she was the one who deprived them of what they perceived as their legitimate claim, all hell broke loose and it was downright cruelty which led to her eventual death.

No finer example of blending of conventionality with an upright strain of individuality could be found than in the character and demeanour of Parbati in *Debdas*. Parbati was quintessentially a Bengali girl whom Tagore termed as one who could only shed tears and remain always at the feet of her man—'*Kandte Sudhu jani, jani eliye podte paye*'.[39] Parbati did all these things as a true and conventional woman, but at the same time she tried desperately to mould and carve out her destiny which she thought was inextricably interlinked with Debdas's. When her marriage was fixed with someone else Parbati, in desperation, rushed to Debdas in the dead of the night to plead with him, itself an act of some daring, but also indicative of her confidence in herself. Debdas, basically a weak character, failed to take a decisive stand. What was more, he pointed out, his parents were dead set against this marriage. Parbati, her pride wounded, flared up and hit back. 'You have your parents, don't I have mine? Don't you think I need their permission to marry?'[40] Again when Debdas asked her 'Have you forgotten me?' At first Parbati was a little flustered then she composed herself and answered 'how could I forget you? From my childhood I have always been scared of you—are you now trying to frighten me? But don't you know me too?' Parbati made it very clear that she was going to marry a much better man and she could never trust a fickle minded immature young man like Debdas. Debdas was dumbfounded, then he uttered: 'Such pride?' 'Why not?' Parbati retorted 'Why can't I have it when you have yours? You are good-looking but devoid of any other quality whereas I am beautiful and have other qualities of character too. Your father is rich, but my father is not exactly a pauper. And what is more within a few days time I can even compete with you in wealth too, you know!'[41]

This outburst on the part of Parbati was no doubt caused by the severe psychological trauma she was going through; nonetheless it demonstrates her capacity to hold on her own; ultimately this is the quality which marked her out as an individual, not merely a stereotypical utterly submissive Bengali girl accepting her fate without a fight.

In the case of two very significant and remarkable characters Anandamayee in *Gora* and Kumu in *Jogajog*, we realize how motherhood in the context of self-identity assumed a singular importance. We envision motherhood in these instances as something at the same time restrictive as well as emancipating. The status and role of mother in itself overshadow all the identities of a woman. It is supposed to be such an all-absorbing, all-pervasive passion, a responsibility that it curtails woman's independent movement and channellizes it to a certain goal—the goal of good motherhood. Motherhood might empower one woman or it might impoverish another. 'The mother's relation with her children takes form within the totality of her life; it depends upon her relations with her husband, her past, her occupation, herself.'[42] For, motherhood, obviously, is not a unidimentional, linear concept; it should rather be viewed with a reference point. One woman might visualize motherhood as transcendence over the trivialities of life, another might feel shackled to the meaninglessness of quotidian existence.

For Anandamayee motherhood did not come very easy—it was not a biological motherhood and because of that it was all the more hard-earned and all the more valuable. It was a tremendously difficult decision to accept Gora as her son. But once she had resolved the issue, it had a cathartic effect on her. It imbued her whole being with a rare strength, with a unique breadth of vision which enabled her to rise above all narrow, partisanal, religious and social bigotry. She repeatedly said that she owed everything, her liberated vision, her non-conformity, unconventionality, to Gora, to her son; once she had accepted Gora as her son, she could not have confined herself to the conservative hidebound world of religious dogmatism and social discrimination. When Gora complained about her nonobservance of ritualistic religious rites, she asserted 'It is because of you, Gora, when you came into my life I decided to forsake all these conventional ceremonial routines. When you embrace a new born baby you realize one does not come to this world with a particular religion. If I try to push anyone out of my life for one's religion or caste, I will have to lose you too.'[43] Gora at that point did not understand the poignancy, the significance of these utterances and refused to eat with his mother and forbade Benoy also to do so. He wanted his mother to get rid of her Christian maid Lakshmi first as a precondition. But Anandamayee was not the one to bend or change her stand so easily:

> I cannot accept what you profess as religious customs or rites, I would rather accept the fact that you would not eat anything touched by me. For me your presence around me would be enough. At least I will be able to see you morning and evening. But I tell you one thing, I will not stop taking anything touched by Lakshmi and that is final.[44]

Anandamayee's non-conformity started as a subjective proposition. She realized for the sake of her son she could not, while keeping her sense of honesty and integrity intact, have stuck to her posture as an orthodox Hindu. She was very clear in her perception about her role in the household. She did not in any way intend to abdicate her liability and obligations to the family. Being in the midst of the mainstream society and community, she did carry on with her usual household duties and at the same time, she maintained her distance ever so carefully. In this context she even minimized the role of Gora's father in her life. His father, always bearing in mind that Gora was not his biological son (adopted at the heyday of his 'youthful aberration'), could not have bequeathed his property to Gora and his real son equally. Anandamayee without a moment's hesitation made it clear that she or her son had no interest in Krishna Dayal's property. He could very easily hand it over to his real son[45] thereby creating a separate world of their own, of the son and the mother.

Anandamayee's subjective decision gradually got transformed into a clarity of vision which transcended the immediacy of the cause; it lifted her high above in the world of objective appraisal of intrinsic human value and worth. And this is a thing which is much more a product of one's inner conviction, as the result of certain amount of exposure at least in the case of Anandamayee. When she was reminded of her high (Brahmin) caste and ancestry, she could answer very easily that she had given up her pretension to and pride in caste hierarchy.

> I know people have branded me irreligious, called me a Christian, I accept and admit everything; why, are not the Christians human beings too? After adopting Gora as my son if I now try to follow all the religious rituals, perhaps I will be accepted in the community but how could I keep my 'dharma'—my belief and conviction intact?[46]

Later on when Benoy was absolutely bewildered about how to resolve the dilemma both Lalita and he faced in their relationship, it was Anandamayee who showed him the way out. Benoy's hesitation arose out of his unwillingness, his inability to hurt Gora's feelings. Gora would be absolutely incensed at the possibility of his marriage with a Brahmo girl and nobody knew it better than Benoy. But Gora's mother had no hesitation whatsoever. 'It is a situation Benoy, she said, when you must forget about Gora. I know Gora would be annoyed and I don't want him to be angry with you. But there is no way out. If you have any respect for Lalita, you must save her from this dishonour' (the whole Brahmo community was abuzz with rumours about Benoy and Lalita's relationship). Benoy's amazement at this remarkable woman was evident in his words 'Ma, you never cease to surprise me. Where did you get this astonishing clarity of judgement? It seems that you do not traverse this earth, it is as if God has given you a pair of wings to rise above all impediments and restrictions.'[47] We encounter the same transparency, the same unorthodox perception when she expressed her sentiment that for the true union of two souls, the role of religion became irrelevant. She did not view it as a necessary precondition to abandon one's religion to make such a union successful or meaningful.[48]

Anandamayee's unique personality, her completely individualistic approach were something inherent in her. It was at the same time a product, at least partially, of the burgeoning middle-class ethos which entailed social mobility, and emergence of nuclear family system, exposure to a not so familiar world outside the strictly demarcated social hierarchy, and interaction with people belonging to different cultures and subcultures. It did contribute to Anandamayee's breadth of vision and realization of her universal human values. In her young age as the wife of a Government employee she spent quite a few years away from home in the distant corners of the country and that was how during the time of the 'Sepoy Mutiny' she adopted Gora. Incidentally, in *Gora* Tagore tried to strike at the roots of sectarian religious orthodoxy whether it appeared among the contemporary Hindu community or among the Brahmos and to evolve the idea of universal brotherhood.

In *Jogajog* Tagore's concern was primarily human relationship and the question of incompatibility in conjugal relations of two widely different persons, man and woman. In a society where male domination was an established fact, subjugation and supplication were women's appointed lot, marital incompatibility and any complaints from the woman's side could come for severest possible censure. 'The basic rules for women's behaviour as expressed in the Laws of Manu insist a woman must constantly worship her husband as a god, even though he is destitute of virtue or a womaniser.'[49] Kumudini decided to stay away from her husband when she realized that there was nothing common between them and they could never establish a meaningful relationship. Madhusudan believed in establishing his rights over his wife on the strength of his legal status as the husband. He intended to dazzle her by vulgar display of his wealth. He had to accept defeat when Kumudini, in her own way, expressed her supreme indifference towards uncouth demonstration of his power. The final severing of any semblance of relationship came with the knowledge of her husband's unsavoury liaison with his widowed sister-in-law.[50] Her determination to seek a purposeful, relevant existence away from her husband in this context was a distinct exception which marked her out as an individual in her own right.

> In *Jogajog* (as we now have it) the large movement of social change is hardly mentioned. Tagore has concentrated on a human problem, but it is a problem, which can arise only in the society where individualism has become a potent force. The elemental problem of the relation between man and woman becomes acute only where social conventions give place to individual claims.[51]

Indeed, this was the teaching Kumu received from her brother, who tried to instil in her mind that a woman should perceive herself as an individual, and should be prepared to fight against the society which refused to recognize women's value. He insisted that Kumu should stay with him: 'You have your rightful place here, you don't have to compromise with anyone to create that space. You will be here in your own right'.[52]

On the strength of this indoctrination Kumu could absolutely effortlessly tell her husband that she was not going back to him, not under any condition or any threat. Her only worry was about her brother. She did not want to be a burden on him. But as long as Kumudini led a shameful existence—of dishonour at her husband's house, her brother would not have any peace of mind. 'And very soon Kumu, we would change our lifestyle. We will have to spend our days as poor people do and you will be the only asset, the only fortune in the midst of our poverty.'[53] But the irony of the situation was such that very soon Bipradas had to change his mind. Kumudini's imminent motherhood forced him to take the most painful decision in his life. Kumu had to go back to her husband. She could not have deprived her unborn child of its legitimate parenthood and he nurtured a faint hope that perhaps Kumu would achieve her fulfilment in motherhood. But for Kumu that was not the end of the road, the eventual death of the prospect of her independent existence. She would come back, she said. 'There are certain things in life which one cannot sacrifice even for one's children. . . . If I cannot preserve my identity as Kumu where does my identity stand as their daughter-in-law?'[54] Unmistakably, her self-identity was much more valuable to her than the identity imposed and ascribed by society and with this poignantly triumphant note about her future she prepared to leave for her husband's home.

The ideal woman was willing to be dependent on men and submissive to them, and she would have a preference for a life restricted to the confines of home. She would be innocent, pure, gentle and self-sacrificing. Possessing no ambitious striving, she would be free of any trace of anger or hostility. More emotional than men, she was also more capable of self-renunciation.[55]

Again, 'By a girl, by a young woman, or even by an aged one, nothing must be done independently, even in her own house'. And 'in childhood a female must be subject to her father, in youth to her husband, and when her lord is dead to her sons. A woman must never be independent'.[56] The first injunction about women's destiny implies a distinctive model for Victorian female personality and the second and the third ones are the prescriptive directions to be found in Manu, the Indian legalist of the seventh century. The time gap, the enormous gaps in culturally conceived typecasts are literally worlds apart; yet all these dictums are trying to put women in a strait-jacket, forcing them to subscribe to the perception which acquired legitimacy in the patriarchal structure of society. The very idea of an 'ideal woman' carries in itself the seed of the strictest possible socialization inducing women to cast off their identity, to be moulded in the frame of stereotyped 'ideal'—mother, daughter or wife—'the entire process of socialization of females is to internalize the concept of dependency which is crippling to the development of their personality',[57] by denying them their sense of individuality.

> Socialization comprises all the social processes by which the young human being comes to know about and believe in the norms and values of the society and also acquire the social roles appropriate to his or her position in it. Our total range of behaviour is shaped by the interaction of these socialization processes with the particular biological potential of the human animal.[58]

Here once again was the seed of gender differentiation. The particular biological potential of the female species of the human animals, it was assumed, was confined to their subordinate roles—the roles society expected them to act out. When from childhood girls are exhorted to emulate Sita or Savitri—obviously they are required to internalize the concept of sexual chastity in mind and body. Implicated in it is the loss of a woman's control of her own body and mind to a man—father, husband, son. Indeed, she had no control over her body even in pursuit of sexual pleasure in common with her husband—her body was for his pleasure, not hers. They are never kept in doubt that they should consider physical chastity as the overwhelmingly important aspect of their being, and their acceptability in society; once they are perceived as having lost it, eternal perdition alone would be their destiny.

> For a woman an act of adultery actually violated her femininity; it was unnatural and irrevocable. This belief that sexual deviancy and its effects were somewhat permanent and unalterable was an important mechanism in the categorization of female sexuality. It was necessary for the boundaries between the permissible and forbidden to appear incontrovertible. For women there could be no movement from one category to another, a fall from virtue was final.[59]

Against the background of this mindset, in the midst of the prevalent social perception, the picture of women viewing chastity as their private concern appraised by their individual perspective, is absolutely overwhelming. It strengthens our faith in the innovativeness of human nature.

The concept of chastity appears to have taken several distinctive forms in the treatment of the three authors we are concerned with. In Bankim it is not even a relevant question. Except for the utterly deviant characters, his heroines or major female characters could never have violated the codes of chastity, not even in thought. We have already dealt with the characters of Suryamukhi and Indira and seen how after a long absence, they could go back to their husbands without much ordeal. Rohini in *Krishnakanter Will*,[60] of course, belonged to a different category. She was a widow, a child widow and was perpetually in a state of tension about her misfortune and deprived existence. First she tried to establish a rapport with Haralal and looked forward to the flowering of a relationship with him. Haralal, to achieve his goal, dangled before her the prospect of widow remarriage and expressed his intention to enter into such an alliance. Very soon Rohini was disillusioned with him and Govindalal, Haralal's cousin, became the object of her love and devotion. But she soon realized that her love for Govindalal could never be expressed to anyone, not even to Govindalal himself;[61] society would in no way entertain the idea of a widow falling in love, it would not allow any relationship to develop between the two. For Rohini it was entirely a question of social propriety, nothing to do with her sense of morality. Not for once did the question of being unchaste or being unfaithful to her dead husband cross her mind. Rohini's conflict could be viewed entirely in the context of social approval. It did not assume a psychological dimension perhaps because of her not-so-developed sense of social morality or because of her early widowhood; the sense of loyalty to her dead husband could not acquire a firm shape. The only reference to her marriage was that 'she was widowed at an early age'.[62] There was thus no dividing line that could be drawn between the two states of her existence—marital and widowhood. If she had missed the experience of one, she felt unconcerned about the other at her own personal level.

The question of chastity with Sarat's women is sometimes a social construction, at others an individual decision depending on the situation or the subject. In the instances which implicate a social construction, the judgement about one's chastity was extraneous to the person, even when internalized by the concerned individual. Biraj in *Biraj Bau*, with ingrained socialization taking deep roots in her psyche considered herself unchaste and polluted as she had left home and had gone to the boat of the local *zamindar*. When she realized the enormity of her folly, she jumped out of the boat into the river—she was not even touched by the 'other man'. But the act of leaving one's home and husband even in a moment of insane anger and frustration was a guilt that the woman could not live down before others; she could only try to atone for it. The tension of being perceived as unchaste by society could hardly be assuaged by her own 'knowledge' of her chastity. Biraj's unshaken faith in the paradigm that unless a woman's body remained unpolluted and was perceived to have remained so, she could not die at the feet of her husband[63] reinforces the verity of the unparalleled significance attached to women's physical chastity as a male construction. Centuries of socialization induced women to accept it as an inviolable maxim, as Biraj did, as a condition of life itself. 'After this [such violation] no Hindu woman should remain alive.'[64]

Savitri in *Charitraheen* found herself in a similar situation and she knew that society's verdict about her status would be that of a *kulata*—one who had placed, her *kula* or *vansha* (family line, ancestry) in shame. Savitri herself accepted and surrendered to this verdict and distanced herself from the man she loved.

> In orthodox Hindu society, perhaps in all orthodox societies a woman who has once transgressed the sexual code is put outside the pale. . . . Physical chastity has, in many societies, been the only test of a woman's worth—whatever her other qualities. They have all been wasted by a single lapse in her sexual life.[65]

Savitri of course had eventually been cleared of any sexual deviancy on her part; nonetheless she was not allowed to occupy any space other than an entirely peripheral and incidental one.

Sarat's *Grihadaha* stands out as a work where *satitva* or physical purity plays a pivotal role, the concept being tossed around from individual to individual, from one situation to another. It was a concept that had taken very strong roots in the mind of man. The characters enmeshed in the situation, where the question of chastity assumed an all-pervading significance, were culturally, socially or educationally wide apart; but at one point they seemed to merge their individual identity, the ultimate right or wrong involving a woman's character, equated with her sexual behaviour. All these characters—Suresh, Kedarbabu, Mahim or Rambabu, all of them were looking at it from different angles, from widely divergent viewpoints, but ultimately arrived at the conclusion that a woman who deviated once, whatever might be the reason, from the path of virtue, could never be forgiven. Mrinal of course was an exception, who maintained that however grave might be the misconduct, forgiveness should never be denied. Mahim expressed his doubt whether a person could be condemned forever for a false step taken by him or her, even though he could not condone his wife's 'deviation'. There was a mild questioning in his mind, of religious sanction to condemnation of women's sexual misdemeanour as demonstrated in Rambabu's horror at the discovery of his unwitting complicity in such misdemeanour: 'The Day of Achala's judgement can wait, Mahim thought, but what sort of religion this orthodox old man subscribes to? His religion seems to have crumbled under the pressure of a falsehood.'[66] Rambabu had assumed that Achala and Suresh were husband and wife as they were living together in his house and later in their own in Dihri. He even had partaken of food prepared by her. And this act, on his part, could now easily be considered as the ultimate fall from the caste hierarchy. After Suresh's death Achala did not agree to perform the last rites stating very plainly that she was not Suresh's wife. The old man did not know how to react to this revelation. The whole world around him lay scattered in pieces. He was shocked beyond words and took the instant decision to go to Varanasi for penance. 'The only thing that created utter din in his ears was that he had lost his religion—he was lost to his immediate society and community—his whole life came to a naught because of this woman.'[67] 'This religion, which instead of providing succour to helpless people itself crumbles against its onslaught—what is the value of it in human life? It does not teach one to be tolerant, to be forgiving; what truth can one arrive at by accepting this religion . . . ?'[68] But the 'deviancy' was still treated as 'deviancy'—to be forgiven rather than accepted as a normal human failing.

Mahim acknowledged that his attempt to run away from the consequences of a false step taken by his wife would be branded and labelled in the same manner but at that very moment, he admitted to himself, he was not fully prepared to handle the whole situation.

Achala had always been trapped in the inner conflict for her divided loyalty. She had been strongly attracted to Suresh but married Mahim whose strength of character and steadfastness held equal attraction for her. Suresh, in spite of his apparently selfless devotion to Achala, did not hesitate for a moment to accuse her of infidelity to her husband. He could very easily proclaim her to be 'not such a *sati-savitri*—such a chaste woman after all'.[69] In Suresh's vision the picture of a *sati-savitri* of a chaste woman was something quite other than Achala, a modern educated Brahmo girl, who did not always unquestioningly subscribe to the orthodox model of devoted wifehood, but whose sexual fidelity nevertheless remained unblemished. Sarat Chandra, in no way, tried to demolish the stereotype, but the way he delineated the characters here in this novel, with sensitivity and sympathy, definitely introduces some sort of nuances, shades in their acceptance of this ultimate stereotype. They did not do it at least without questioning the authenticity of the models thus presented. Achala herself was the prime example of this questioning mind. Achala, no doubt, carried all along the guilt of her divided loyalty; however, one positively feels that but for Suresh's passionate impetuosity, her sentiment would have remained at the stage of a very pleasant and caring friendship. Nonetheless at one point she did raise questions about the pretences involving the theory of life-long (or extending even beyond) devotion of a woman to one man only. 'In their society (that is, Brahmo society) widows are allowed to marry again. It is unlike Hindu society where women had to carry the burden of wifehood through life and death. This sort of closed-mindedness which leashes a woman to remain steadfast to one man only was not expected of her.' She was guilty of course, guilty of recognizing, at least of thinking of the possibility of another man as her husband when her real husband was still alive, but this feeling did not entail any sense of sin or fear of penance in the life after death.[70] This liberation from orthodoxy, B.B. Majumdar, in a different context, attributed to the changing perception in society, 'the degree of transformation of the society in first four decades of the present century'.[71]

On another occasion Achala argued with Mrinal on the theme of female chastity and purity and tried very hard to impress upon her that Mrinal's *dharma* was the *dharma* which suffered from oppression and duplicity whereas her's was more sensible and rational.

> Well, if you think you have been most assiduously trained by your society to observe this path of correct behaviour, then how do you justify all these restrictions which tend to isolate women from the outside world? When you are left with no choice but to stick to your path of '*satitva*' and you cannot deviate from it even if you try to, how do you test your devotion to the concept without any outside temptation, provocation or challenge?

Mrinal's reaction to this was very simple; she said 'for you, marriage is something of a social contract, but for us marriage is made in heaven. You can argue about what is good and what is bad in this system, and accordingly change your opinion, but for us it is part of our upbringing, our entity and our codes of morality which cannot be changed.'[72] But coming down to brass tacks, when Achala had to compromise her sense of right and wrong, when ultimately she had to compromise her chastity which she believed was her *atyayya satidharama*—unforsaken sense of physical purity—and which would have saved her, she was not much different from Mrinal. After her sexual surrender to Suresh she was completely devastated, and the imprint of it was clearly visible the morning after that fateful night in 'her deathly pale face, deep dark shadow under her eyes and stream of tears flowing down her stricken cheeks'.[73]

This in a way is the hub: Sarat was not entirely convinced of this argument of women's chastity as a narrative; but he would not boldly challenge it as cultural inheritance, as *samskara* and he did not see the two as inter-related.

The conflict between a sense of social morality and one of individual morality has been graphically portrayed in many of the protagonists in Sarat. In Achala the received sense of honour vanquished her inner inquisitiveness and her experimentation with her own body and emotions. She never could expose her true identity to her affectionate host Rambabu and she decided to carry on with the deceit they were perpetuating and entered Suresh's bedroom and her 'ultimate doom'. What she could not say was 'Rambabu, wish me to be honest at least once before you. So far you have known me as a chaste, respectable woman, but I am no such thing and let me have the courage to face the reality and be condemned as a woman of uncertain virtue.'[74] The agony of this conflict has clearly been expressed in Kedarbabu's reaction to his daughter's elopement. In public, he pronounced it to be an unforgivable crime and preferred his daughter's death to such a disgrace. But in the privacy of his solitude and grief he broke down and was prepared to accept her back and even leave home in the process.[75]

The same dichotomy between social and individual morality is more emphatically manifest in two female characters, Abhaya and Rajlakshmi in *Shrikanta*. Both of them could very easily be termed deviants, for they remained somewhat outside the mainstream society, although both were determined to make something worthwhile out of their unconventional relationships. Rajlakshmi was quite sure about her status as a successful courtesan and as someone who commanded popularity and prestige in her own sphere, had enough confidence to assert her identity and she did not find anything amiss in her relationship with Shrikanta 'If people call it "living in sin", let them, I would rather accept this than doing a hundred pious deeds, and if it is assumed as going against religion then I would leave religion alone and welcome it.'[76] Once while narrating her past life to Shrikanta, she commented 'Hundreds of men and women have exchanged marriage vows from time immemorial, sacred is their love and so is their relationship, but this Rajlakshmi of yours, now a "fallen woman" a "Kulota" has loved you all her life and loved you so much that nobody can come near it.'[77] This defiance of the accepted social norms, confidence in being right in taking her own decision invested Rajlakshmi's character with a rare strength, no doubt, but in her devotion to Shrikanta she was consciously or unconsciously repeating the *patibrata* syndrome with some out of the ordinary elements thrown in. Abhaya's search for identity is genuinely spectacular because of the enormity of the struggle, multipronged conflict of conscience which went in behind the scene to articulate it. Abhaya's decision to spend the rest of her life with Rohini can be viewed as the ultimate triumph of her search for identity in a finely honed individual way.

Abhaya went to Burma to establish her identity as her husband's wife and failing there she tried to seek out an alternative identity and in the course of this search she discovered herself, her sense of self. In her desperate search for personal fulfilment, the element of unconventionality and non-conformity, in addition to her self-confidence, assumed the form of an open challenge in which the purity of love and unblemished truthfulness were being appropriated in opposition to convention: 'Whatever you might call me or term my children as, one thing I know very clearly, my children born out of our pure and genuine love, would not in anyway be inferior to anyone in this world. Truth would be their only asset and that is the only thing they will inherit from their parents.'[78]

Shrikanta's mumbled philosophizing that men's actions and women's could not be measured on the same scale and society would disintegrate if its members followed their own biddings was then a very authentic representation of patriarchal society's concerns. Abhaya was left in no doubt that in Hindu society she or her children had no place of their own and she was obliged to think of Muslim society, where she knew she would be quite welcome. Faced with the choice of conformity or exclusion, Abhaya's final statement in this context underscores the determined assertion of her individuality most succinctly:

> But I am not going out of this society. With all my misfortune, all the burden of my bad name and reputation, I will remain here in the midst of you all. I would try to raise my children as real human beings. I would like to see what is more important, their birth, how and where they were born or their real worth, their intrinsic value as human beings.[79]

The concept of chastity in Tagore assumes psychological rather than sociological overtones. It becomes multi-dimensional with a pronounced stress on individualistic images as well as notions. Society, in his characters' sphere of life apparently ceased to play much too decisive a role. For illustration, we shall deal with three of his characters: Binodini in *Chokher Bali*, Kumudini in *Jogajog* and Urmimala in *Dui Bon*. Violation of codes of chastity, albeit mental, in the case of Urmimala, the sense of outraged chastity in Kumudini and subversion of the accepted norms of *sativa* by Binodini were all feelings and acts independent of social sanction. Socialization of course remained a strong factor. Urmimala, in spite of her liberal upbringing and high education could not release herself completely from the hold it had on female psyche. 'Urmi tells herself very sternly I *will have to be true*, true to my word.' Her father had arranged her betrothal with Nirad and to be unfaithful to it was like violating the codes of chastity for her.[80] She was fascinated by Shashanka, her elder sister's husband and could not deny the inexorable pull of attraction towards him. She was also aware of Shashanka's partiality towards her and she felt guilty—guilty of being unfaithful to her betrothed as well as to her father's wishes. Interestingly, her feeling of guilt did not extend to her relationship with her elder sister. It was at least not uppermost in her mind. She never felt that her action might amount to some sort of injustice or betrayal of the faith her sister posited in her. There is a reflection here of the empirical reality of Bengali kinship structure in which a relationship with sexual undertones or marriage with elder sister's husband is not disapproved of. At the end of the story, Urmi prepares to sail to England, an act most unorthodox on the part of men, and almost beyond belief on the part of a young girl. Clearly, between Sarat and Tagore the very modalities of resolving conflicts around women's sexuality had crossed unassailable barriers, itself a testimony to the growing assertion of their self-identity.

How society as the arbiter of individual morality was receding from its earlier position, at least in the urban milieu, is quite explicit in the way Mahendra and Binodini were conducting their affair. She appeared to be slightly uncomfortable about her association with Mahendra in the presence of her kinsfolks at her in-law's village. She agreed to leave the village along with Mahendra but refused to allow him to travel in the same coach with her on their way to the railway station.[81] Once in Calcutta, the combination of insular existence of the city-dwellers and the nuclear family system blunted the edge of social sanctions, so pronounced in villages. The question of chastity where Binodini was involved turns out to be an emotional and psychological problem. In the scheme of things evolved by her, her deceased husband had lost his relevance completely, as far as she was concerned.

Between Mahendra and Behari, she always felt much more strongly attracted towards Behari, but circumstances linked her fate with Mahendra's. As the final denouement of the story she most graciously took leave of Asha and Mahendra. She had already rejected the marriage proposal from Behari assuring him that she would rather wait for her next birth to have him as her husband, thereby inverting completely the notion of chaste women's devotion to her '*Pati Param Guru*' and to one man only in life as well as in death, and in life after death.[82] If her widowhood yet came in the way of her acceptance of Behari's proposal, it was owing to her concern for his honour. The story itself is rather weak in craftsmanship, but it does delineate the departures from values, even if not quite robustly.

The complexity of Kumudini's situation was quite overwhelming. Kumudini's model husband was shaped and sustained by the legendary figures of Hindu mythology, more so by the heroes of the Sanskrit literature *Raghuvansha* and *Kumarasambhava*. The only male figure in her conscious world was that of her brother Bipradas, accomplished, enlightened and erudite. Marriage to her was the union of two like-minded individuals, a relationship that would brook no shortfalls in the ideals she had set-up. But the reality she encountered on her first meeting with her husband was most distressing as she realized that the cultural gulf between them was almost unbridgeable 'Madhusudan is a successful man of the world, vulgar, coarse and masterful. He seeks to possess Kumudini not because he loves her but as an assertion of victory in family rivalry.'[83] Kumudini came to her husband's house with all the faith in the Hindu woman's duties towards her husband. Madhusudan, with his crudity and meanness of mind became the most insurmountable barrier between the two. Kumudini tried desperately to surrender to her husband's will and wanted some more time to prepare herself for it. But Madhusudan, in his arrogant impatience refused to wait and invaded her privacy. This sexual assault left Kumudini a complete mental wreck. The image of her, the morning after that night of atrocity, was a reminder of a victim of rape—with 'red, swollen eyes, a face drained of all colour and life'.[84] Indeed Kumudini too perceived the experience in the same image. Her dream shattered, she took refuge in accepting the marriage as a divine sanction and to make it work at least for appearances sake—both values derived again from classical Hindu idiom. Inside, she was still unreconciled to what struck her as an 'impurity', a sense of the violation of her chastity, as in rape.[85] Kumudini was thus trying to redefine this concept of chastity in the context of conjugal relationship: chastity, for her was not interchangeable with the husband's monopoly over the wife's sexuality; it was the purity of her body and sensibility in her own personal world, the violation of which wounded her in or outside the marriage.

Here in a way Kumudini was rather unconsciously, reiterating

> . . . an extension of the general principle of bodily integrity or bodily self-determination to the notion that women must be able to control their own bodies and procreative capacities—that is, the reproductive and sexual uses to which their bodies are put . . . dimensions of reproduction, . . . rooted in the conceptual framework of 'natural rights'. . . .[86]

In Kumudini's as in other women's world-view chastity was not merely a phenomenon of the female body: the more important facet of it was one of sensibility. Bharati in *Patherdabi* had accepted Apurba as her husband and found herself enmeshed in a complicated situation. Apurba hailed from an orthodox high caste Hindu family and Bharati, a Christian, could not in any way be optimistic about their union. But Bharati had loved Apurba and once she had loved a man, she could not have accepted anyone else as her husband and that was the basic assumption of a woman's spiritual chastity. 'I am not Nabotara (another female character in the novel, who betrayed her beloved); I know I have made a mistake, but there is no way to correct it now. I had thought of him as my husband once. . . .'[87] The inevitability of the conclusion that he alone would be her husband for her life's span gets enhanced emphasis from the part of the sentence that is left hanging. Bharati's Christian denomination hardly veils this encompassing cultural ethos following the codes of conduct laid down by Hindu society. But Sabyasachi, perhaps unconsciously reflecting the vision of a liberal, upper caste Hindu male, saw it as a basic quality of Bengal's women, irrespective of religious traditions, something invaluable, transcending all misfortunes and maladies of the community. 'Nabotaras are there, so are the Bharatis and there lies our strength. You will never get anything comparable to this in the whole world.'[88] This mode of Sabyasachi's identity gets into highlight when in the next breath he denounces all traditions of religion, society and community to doom, save the tradition of women's fidelity to this one ideal, for he saw no inconsistency between the two sentiments. This ambivalence was embedded in the middle class *bhadralok* psyche. Most liberal minds faltered and hesitated when faced with the question of women's individual choice and subscribed merrily to the conventional ethos. The decision on the part of Bharati aids clearly a culturally determined decision, part of Hindu ethos to be found in folklore and mythology; such commitment is expected of women; they had been socialized into it.

A situation similar to it arose when Bijaya[89] tried to sort out the tangle of relationship with two men in her life. Bijaya was formally engaged to Bilash but Naren was the man she had fallen in love with, and she could not think of anyone else as her husband. Earlier getting married to Bilash was not a very hard decision. 'But now even the possibility of being touched by someone else except that one person was a matter of grave shame, as if she was committing some sin.'[90] It was this feeling of 'sinfulness' that was the reverse side of 'chastity'. Bijaya had fallen in love with Naren, and to love one and to marry someone else amounted to violating codes of chastity. She had pledged her body sexually as well her soul to Naren and it was a psychological and spiritual relationship as much as it was physical.

The notion of individuality as we perceive it now, was not in existence at the time we are dealing with, and women's individuality was a far cry from what it is now. Women, subjected to the regimentation of stereotypical mould, were not allowed, much less encouraged to express their independent views. Nevertheless women of various categories as we have already seen exhibited certain amount of what could be called 'exploration of the self' and their actions had often been dictated by their personal sense of what was right and what was wrong, a sense that often brought them out of step with societal diktats.

NOTES AND REFERENCES

1. Simone de Beauvoir, *The Second Sex*, tr. H.M. Parshley, London: Picador, 1988, p. 16.
2. Sudhir Kakar, *The Inner World: A Psycho-analytic Study of Childhood and Society in India,* New Delhi: OUP, 1992, p. 79.
3. Rabindranath Tagore, '*Streer Patra*', pp. 638-9.
4. *Shrikanta, Charitraheen* and *Sheshprashna.*
5. Sarat Chatterjee, *Shrikanta,* p. 503.
6. Sarat Chatterjee in his essay 'Narir Mulya' (Woman's Worth) raised the same question, 'The most admirable attribute in a woman is her chastity: This is an accepted truth in all societies as it is the most gratifying object of consumption for men of all ages. To disobey one's husband or to disregard him is most deplorable in a woman's character and this has been discussed threadbare from the time of our mythology and legends, in various forms of arguments and counter arguments and all this has been done for the benefit of women. Men, on the other hand, were not born to suffer under any such restrictions. In English the term "chastity"

could equally be applicable to both men and women. "Satitva" is a word with connotation relevant only to women', p. 948.

7. *Shrikanta*, p. 504.
8. Ramsay Muir, in *Introduction to Indian Nationality* by R.N. Gilchrist, as quoted in M.M. Urquhart, *Women of Bengal*, Calcutta: Association Press, 1927, p. 63.
9. *Charitraheen*, p. 230.
10. Ibid., p. 229.
11. Kalpana Bardhan, 'Women and Feminism in a Stratified Society', in Sally J.M. Sutherland, ed., *Bridging Worlds*, Oxford: OUP, 1991, p. 174.
12. Sarat Chatterjee, '*Sheshprashna*', p. 360.
13. Ibid., p. 247.
14. Ibid., p. 268.
15. Ibid., p. 246.
16. Ibid., p. 276.
17. 'Streer Patra', p. 636.
18. Ibid., p. 647.
19. Erving Goffman, *Asylums*, p. 28.
20. Sudhir Chandra in his *The Oppressive Present* has taken note of this change and asserts 'The pace of change, though slow seems visible'. This change, he points out, could be seen in the attitudes towards the widows, as manifested from Bankim to Tagore. 'The struggling Hindu widow in *Krishnakanter Will* had been scotched by the moralist in Bankim. In Tagore's *Chokher Bali* she is, for the first time, a person in her own right.' And 'at least her author stands by her', p. 114.
21. Natalie Zemon Davis, 'Boundaries and Sense of Self in Sixteenth Centuries France', in Thomas C. Heller et al., eds., *Reconstructing Individualism*, Stanford: Stanford University Press, 1986, p. 53.
22. 'Streer Patra', p. 647.
23. Tagore, 'Haimanti' (short story).
24. B.B. Majumdar, *Heroines of Tagore: A Study in the transformation of Indian Society*, Calcutta: Firma K.L. Mukhopadhyaya, 1968, p. 94.
25. Ibid., p. 95.
26. Haimanti's husband's 'helplessness' and the term 'victim' would definitely be frowned upon by many 'right thinking' people. Kalpana Bardhan in her 'Introduction' to *Of Women, Outcasts, Peasant and Rebels: A Selection of Bengali Short Stories* edited and translated and with an Introduction by Kalpana Bardhan, Berkeley: University of California Press, 1990 has seen him as a 'victim' (9-17), whereas Arati Rao in her review article '(Re-writing women's wor(l)ds: Facts and Fiction', in *South Asia Bulletin*, vol. XI, no. 1+2 (1991) questions the relevance of the term and frowns upon any 'concession' being made to a male!
27. Usha Nilsson, 'Women in Contemporary Indian literature', in Sally J.M.

Sutherland, ed., *Bridging Worlds: Studies on Women in South Asia*, Oxford: OUP, 1991, pp. 108-9.

28. Sarat Chatterjee, *Patherdabi*, p. 162.
29. Tagore, *Gora*, p. 33.
30. Ibid., p. 156.
31. Meenakshi Mukherjee, *Realism and Reality: The Novel and Society in India*, New Delhi: OUP, 1985, p. 69.
32. Usha Nilsson, 'Women in Contemporary Indian Literature', in Salley J.M. Sutherland, ed., *Bridging Worlds*, p. 109.
33. Bankim Chatterjee, *Bishabriksha*, p. 219.
34. Bankim Chatterjee, *Indira*.
35. *Debichoudhurani*, p. 678.
36. Ibid., p. 652.
37. Sarat Chatterjee, *Bamuner Meye*, p. 651.
38. Tagore, 'Dena Paona', p. 33.
39. Tagore, 'Banshiwala', *Shyamali* (Sanchaita Visva Bharati edn. VI), p. 715.
40. Sarat Chatterjee, *Debdas*, p. 38.
41. Ibid.
42. Simone de Beauvoir, *Second Sex*, p. 537.
43. *Gora*, p. 13.
44. Ibid., p. 14.
45. Ibid., p. 24.
46. Ibid., pp. 24-5.
47. Ibid., p. 228.
48. Ibid., p. 270.
49. Neera Desai and Maithreyee Krishnaraj, *Women and Society in India*, Delhi: Ajanta Publication, 1987, p. 28. Also see Meredith Borthwick, *The Changing Role of Women in Bengal (1849-1905)*, Princeton: Princeton University Press, 1984, p. 109.
50. '*Bhabhi*' or sister-in-law, in the context of Bengali society may mean the wife of a distant cousin, as is the case here.
51. Humayun Kabir, *The Bengali Novel*, pp. 56-7.
52. *Jogajog*, p. 689.
53. Ibid., p. 706.
54. Ibid., p. 710.
55. Debora Gorham, *The Victorian Girl and the Feminine Ideal*, London and Canberra: Croom Helm, 1982, p. 5.
56. Wm. Theodore de Bary, *Sources of Indian Tradition*, vol. I, New York, 1958 as quoted in Sally J.M. Sutherland, ed., *Bridging Worlds*, Oxford: OUP, 1991, pp. 102-3.
57. Neera Desai and M. Krishnaraj, *Women and Society in India*, Delhi: Ajanta Publication, 1987, p. 202.
58. This is a working definition of socialization given by William J. Good

in his *The Family* (2nd edn.), Delhi: Prentice-Hall, 1987, pp. 20-1. Its value rests in clarity, even if it weighs somewhat heavily towards absolute 'conditioning' of human individual.

59. Lynda Nead, *Myths of Sexuality: Representation of Women in Victorian Britain*, p. 49.
60. Bankim Chatterjee, *Krishnakanter Will.*
61. Ibid., p. 438
62. Ibid., p. 430
63. Sarat Chatterjee, *Biraj Bau*, p. 102.
64. Ibid., p. 104.
65. H. Kabir, *The Bengali Novel*, pp. 88-9.
66. *Gribadaha*, p. 606.
67. Ibid., p. 603.
68. Ibid., p. 606.
69. Ibid., p. 544.
70. Ibid., p. 570.
71. B.B. Majumdar, *Heroines of Tagore*, p. 122.
72. *Gribadaha*, p. 592.
73. Ibid., p. 575.
74. Ibid.
75. Ibid., pp. 584-5.
76. *Shrikanta*, p. 691.
77. Ibid., p. 710.
78. *Charitraheen*, p. 505.
79. Ibid., p. 506.
80. Tagore, *Dui Bon*, p. 448.
81. *Chokher Bali*, pp. 327-8.
82. Ibid., p. 373.
83. H. Kabir, *The Bengali Novel*, pp. 56-7.
84. Tagore, *Jogajog*, p. 634.
85. Ibid.
86. Rosalind Pollack Petchesky, 'Reproduction Freedom: Beyond Woman's Right to Choose', in Catherine R. Stimpson and Ethel Spector Parson, eds., *Women, Sex and Sexuality*, Chicago and London: University of Chicago Press, 1980, pp. 93-4.
87. *Patherdabi*, p. 178.
88. Ibid., p. 174.
89. Sarat, *Datta.*
90. Ibid., p. 377.

CHAPTER 5

Conclusion

All received perceptions of orthodox patriarchal society deny any kind of autonomous space, even physical space, to women in the family's context which in turn is enlarged on to social space. The socialization of the female child which prompts her to believe that her survival depends upon space primarily occupied by men, begins early. The arrival of the daughter coincides with the vision of her marriage—she is a bird of passage from the moment of her birth, until she relieves her parents of her physical and emotional presence by settling down in the next locale of her passage—the in-laws. In one of his moving Hindi songs Amir Khusrau gives voice to this very status of bird of passage for the girl child where the daughter laments that she is forever a guest in her natal home, and the mother admits with sadness that this indeed is so. The daughter, in another song, does not try to make secret of the trace of sorrow as she opens her heart to her father that she is like a bird on his terrace, to fly away in whichever direction he whisked her. But lament does not come in the way of her acceptance of her destiny. After marriage when women are transported to their husband's home, the only space they can expect is the one that is granted to their husbands, and that too according to the status their husbands occupy in the household. It is a shared space where a woman is always an inferior partner. In case of her husband's absence—temporary or long-term—she tends to lose even that space, and it contracts even further if she were to become a widow. Similarly, women's social or moral space also perches precariously on the male constructed paradigm of the 'correct' behavioural norm laid down for them. For a woman even one fall in a lifetime is a perpetual banishment from social space. One step against the values of the concerned social order, taken wittingly or otherwise, spells irreversible moral degradation for the woman.

All this is given to us by the weight of received wisdom. To the extent that we have attempted to go a step beyond this wisdom, this is done in an exploratory kind of way in disaggregating the collectives and stereotypes implicit in this vision and breaking them down to the individual as the irreducible entity. Within the collective, the person is not merely an inert, passive object of structured domination; within the confines of the structure, she is also a subject, an active agent out to corrode the structural confines through a range of strategies and seek some sort of individualized fulfilment of her life and locate some virtue in it.

Our concern here has not been with a single field (women's history) but with several, indeed all fields, in which women are considered a constituent, once marginalized in history and society as a whole. We may need different analytical tools, concepts, and above all a different vision in order to investigate and identify these problematics; and, for sure, we need to use the existing tools and concepts in a new way.[1] This work is an exploration in this perspective. We have taken as our case study the familiar characters—wives, mothers and other women coming from the margins of society, like prostitutes—showing them in a different light 'to replace the dominant image of a lowly, neglected and negligible housewife, beaten and humiliated, with that of a rebellious woman of the people, active and strong, the guardian of the family's means of subsistence, in control of the family budget, at the heart of the urban sphere'.[2] We have here ventured to include along with the housewives and the domestic sphere, the women who are condemned forever to the black holes of existence—the so-called fallen women or the prostitutes. From their severely restricted social and physical status, they could extend their influence and acquire some power and create space for themselves—even in the presentation of their images by men authors. Space here clearly coincides with social and moral dimensions and visualizes dramatic change in women's perceptions of themselves while asserting their individuality and a separate identity. Individuality, as we have already discussed and emphasized, is a concept not easily associated with traditionally constructed notion of women's role and status. When the still venerated Manu, the law-giver, states that women should be given no freedom under any circumstance[3] and 'when a woman is joined with her husband in accordance with the rules, she takes on the very same qualities that he has, *just like the river flowing down into the ocean*'[4] (emphasis added), he very clearly denies women a separate identity which is undefined by their relationship with men, expecting them to merge their individual identity with that of their men. But in spite of all these restrictive measures and circumscribed female existence, we do see women rising above their seemingly insurmountable socio-psychological impediments, seeking out their own identity, their sense of the self, sometimes without external assistance and occasionally with help from the men themselves. They are not extraordinary women, but the most familiar, most quotidian, placed in everyday contexts within the household next door.

In the studies of the sociology of literature, or of literary criticism, the primary concern of most writers has been the mapping of heterosexual relationships in fiction. Patriarchal parameters have allowed little space for the analysis of inter-female bonds. Indeed, women have characteristically been branded as one another's worst enemies, for, after all, women's fickleness and jealousy had long been the target for the satirists, as has often been encountered in popular literature. But interestingly enough, in the course of my research, I encountered an impressive number of instances where the bonds of emotional empathy between women had been the bedrock of interpersonal relationships, contrary to the surface assumption of general animosity and bickering reigning supreme amongst female characters.

It is my intention to extend the scope of this exploration by, paradoxically, narrowing down its focus: my attempt at exposition in this context would be to trace the existence of genuine compassion and deep understanding emerging out of a 'complex and primary allegiance between women'. In my primary sources women are located at differential stages of relative deprivation of power; yet they tend to show a remarkable sense of solidarity with their less fortunate sisters and thus underscore the need for and importance of nurturing supportive female presence. What makes such a study more engaging is that the nature of such female-female friendships is not necessarily univocal, characterized by sympathetic bonding between women. The subject often tends to become polysemous. Women may endorse patriarchal values in males, yet, in a subtle way they subvert them in the female spaces of their world. Further, even in these female spaces female friendships abound with contradictory emotions such as sympathy and rivalry, love and jealousy, etc. This, however, may not indicate a dilution of the intensity and profundity of the relationships. My endeavour, hereafter, would be to explore the theme in three contexts: the mother and daughter; the widow and other members of the family; and the world of the courtesan.

One of the most abiding and poignant female bonds which can exist is the mother and daughter relationship and here we enter the nature-centred female world with its multi-faceted potential. In a society where women have been assigned a subordinate position it is not difficult to imagine the locus of the female child. Her mother in turn is filled with an acute sense of guilt, self-reproach, and helplessness from the moment the child is born. (Guilt because of having given birth to a daughter whom the patriarchal structure will perceive as a life-long liability; and helplessness and frustration because the mother's affection for the daughter still remains in tact and yet she is unable to redress wrongs done to her child.)

The female child herself begins to feel the stifling discrimination that is her fate which neither she nor her mother can even moderate. This shared feeling of guilt and frustration reinforces the bond of affection between them and consequently a sense of perceptive, yet quiet insight in their mutual life situations. We have, of course, considered and dealt with this facet at some length in our chapter on interpersonal relationships.

Widows, the subject of our second theme, are at the bottom of the heap. The social rejection of widows in the upper class Hindu milieu expresses itself in their marginalization. They are socially differentiated by prescribed behaviour. Their normative codes of conduct are generally enforced by other female members of the family and its networks. Yet, within the large avenues of prescriptive and proscriptive behaviours, there is, we have seen, the existence of mutually reinforced ties of perceptive understanding and quiet comforting of widows by other women. They do not so often question the legitimacy of the norms, but help to soften their blows somewhat.

Finally, the courtesans within *kothas* (their residence and performance locales which enclose an entire world within their walls). Banished from the mainstream of female society as individuals, these women create a world of their own. Within the context of this parallel and exclusive society of women, they share an existence of a high sense of camaraderie, wit, teasing and affectionate interaction with a host of other women providing a nurturing ambience complete in itself. They find a measure of confidence and self-sufficiency in their mutual friendship and thus substitute the familial or societal support system which they normally miss in their segregated passage of life. The sheer presence of characters cited so far, and the possibility of their very existence in the context of Bengal itself constitutes a powerful question. In the backdrop of a regional society ridden with the problems of widow remarriage, atrocities perpetrated against them in the name of society and religious morality and ethics, lives of the highest number of widows in the country going up in flames on their husband's funeral pyres, vociferous and vehement protests against the Age of Consent Bill, the question becomes all the more emphatic. This manifestation of quiet strength, of inner power in the female characters, most of them nothing but conventional, and some others truly unconventional, created by male authors leaves behind a puzzling question. To contextualize this question, we cannot possibly put forward the argument that this phenomenon is nothing but the expression of inherent and ingrained surrender to the concept of Mother-cult. Bengali men, culturally and historically, have for long been great devotees of the manifestation of supreme power in the form of Mother Goddess(es). Mothers, or women generally, were envisioned as the ultimate repository of this unique spiritual power. This sort of psycho-socio-cultural perspective might have contributed, to a great extent, to the framing of the powerful female characters. And there might have remained a wide gap between what was and what should have been, between the world of imagination and the realm of hard reality. Even so, to explain away the whole episode exclusively on the basis of this argument would perhaps be much too simplistic. The perfect intermingling of the cult of Mother Goddess with the nationalist imagination, an early rendering of it we find in Bankim's '*Ma ja chhilen*' (what mother once was), '*Ma ja haiachhen*' (what mother now is) and '*Ma ja hoiben*' (what mother would transform herself into). Here Mother is the mirror of the motherland, the nation. Partha Chatterjee, in his *The Nation and its Fragments* has deliberated, in a most erudite fashion, upon the question of appropriating the image of woman as the sole arbiter of all that is good and great in Indian culture and tradition in the nationalist agenda. In doing so, he has argued, nationalism initiated a 'new patriarchy' and a new tradition—'reformed, reconstructed, fortified against charges of barbarism and irrationalism',[5] wherein women with infinite spiritual power and virtue were accorded a superiority not only to the 'unreformed' lower class native females but to the educated yet Westernized women too.

> The home was the principal site for expressing the spiritual quality of the national culture, and women must take the main responsibility for protecting and nurturing this quality. No matter what the changes in the external conditions of life for women, they must not lose their essentially spiritual (that is, feminine) virtues; they must not, in other words, become essentially Westernized.[6]

Nothing, perhaps, could have underlined the ambivalence embedded in middle class elite attitude towards women more succinctly as has been done here. It is of this ambivalence, which, perhaps, in nationalist trajectory had its own compulsion, we have talked so often and at some length in our text. Bengali male under the colonial rule experienced the most ignominious humiliation in the form of constant and persistent challenge to his masculinity posed by the alien superior power. He had forever been branded as weak and effeminate, lacking in courage and physical strength. This image gained currency to the extent of finding an echo in indigenous art and literature. Not in a position to contradict or countermand this hypothesis in the outside world, the Bengali male gaze turned towards the inner chamber, inhabited by women and was engaged in constructing and refashioning an image of empowered woman, a 'heroic female figure who is seemingly autonomous and in control.'[7] This attempt was, in all probability, directed as a device of self-defence and a way to share the glory attributed to powerful female figure and thus retrieve some of the lost ground.

NOTES AND REFERENCES

1. For a perception of this methodological genre, see Sylvie Vande-Casteele-Schweitzer and Daniele Voldman, 'The Oral Sources for Women's History', in Michelle Perrot, ed., *Writing Women's History*, p. 48.
2. Michelle Perrot, 'Women, Power and History', in ibid., p. 163.
3. Manu, *The Laws of Manu*, verse 9: 3, p. 197.
4. Ibid., verse 9: 22, p. 199.
5. Partha Chatterjee, *The Nation and its Fragments*, p. 127.
6. Ibid., p. 126.
7. Indira Choudhury, *The Frail Hero and Virile History: Gender and Politics of Culture in Colonial Bengal*, New Delhi: OUP, 1998, p. 7.

APPENDIX

Summary of Novels

Indira (1873)

Indira, daughter of a wealthy *zamindar*, was kidnapped by a band of robbers on her way to her husband's home and was left alone in wilderness after they had robbed her of all her jewellery and other precious things. Without her attendants and her companions around, she could neither reach her father's house nor her husband's as she had no idea how to travel from the place where she had been abandoned by the robbers. As a desperate move, she sought employment as a cook in a *bhadralok* household and the daughter-in-law of the house very soon struck a friendship with her, being of the same age. With the help of the kindly gentleman and his family she could reach Calcutta, where she met her husband. But meeting him and being accepted by him and his family were two entirely different things. After some skilful manoeuvring, in which she was assisted and encouraged by her friend and her husband, she could establish her identity and achieve her objective.

Bishabriksha (1873)

The eternal triangle of love played by cupid is at the centre of *Bishabriksha*. Nagendra and Suryamukhi are the main protagonists—Kundanandini is a mere appendage, a plaything in the hands of destiny to further the complexity of the plot after a rather innocuous start of the novel. Nagendra and Suryamukhi, supposedly an ideal couple with perfect understanding between themselves adopted Kunda, an orphan and destitute, and got her married to a man of their choice. Things started happening after the death of this man. Widowed, once again she came back to her benefactors. Nagendra suddenly woke up to the beauty, innocence and vulnerability of the young widow, and could not resist the attraction and decided to marry her. Widow remarriage had by then become at least legally accepted. Suryamukhi, out of her sense of injured pride and of acquiescence to her husband's wishes, consented, but left home after the wedding. It proved to be a rather rude shock for Nagendra and he on his part followed suit in search of Suryamukhi. After journeying to and fro, both of them ultimately came back home. Kunda realized that her love as well as her life was superfluous in the whole scheme of things and as a way out committed suicide. In her death all the angular projections were rounded off and the story came to a desired end.

Krishnakanter Will (1878)

Krishna Kanta, an affluent householder, had two sons and a nephew to inherit his property after his death. He also had a younger brother who had died early leaving a young son behind. Krishna Kanta's property was the fruit of his and his younger brother's joint venture and he wanted to bequeath half his property to Govindalal, his nephew. Haralal, Krishna Kanta's elder son, raised objection to this arrangement. His enraged father made a new will depriving him even of what he had conceived of as his rightful share. Haralal, in an attempt to jeopardize his father's intention sought outside help and approached Rohini, the child widow, leading a life of emotional and sexual deprivation, to help him change the will made by his father. Haralal persuaded Rohini to change the will with her nimble fingered expertise and substitute a forged one for the real thing. Rohini agreed, her reward being the promise of marriage with Haralal. But very soon she discovered the hoax played upon her by Haralal and Rohini decided to take back the original will and leave it in Krishna Kanta's cupboard. This time over, luck failed her and she was caught and humiliated. She did not find any alternative open to her except suicide. She was, of course, eventually saved by none other than Govindalal, the hero of the story. Govindalal, in turn, lost himself to her charm and beauty, and the story of her distress and misfortune had a very deep impact on his mind. The inevitable followed: Govindalal started neglecting his young wife Bhramar and ultimately eloped with Rohini. The tragic end came when Bhramar died after much suffering and Rohini was murdered by Govindalal as a just punishment for her infidelity. For Govindalal it was a life of repentance and renunciation as long as he survived.

Debichoudhurani (1884)

In *Debichoudhurani,* Bankim delineated the amazing transformation of a helpless girl into an all-powerful accomplished leader of a socio-religious group of outlawed followers. Prafulla, deserted by her husband, Brajeshwar, and disowned by her in-laws, came into contact with Bhawani Pathak, so far the chief of the group and it was he who perceived in her the elements of head and heart which go to make a leader and trained her as his successor. This is the story of a woman, who, after journeying through all the exotic experiences of life, preferred to come back to the old and familiar incarnation of wifehood and achieve life's fulfilment in assuming the role of a strong, determined and purposeful housewife. Other characters adding extra dimensions to the theme are Prafulla's husband Brajeshwar, her parents-in-law and her co-wives, Sagar and Nayan. Amongst them all, Sagar is the one who could leave some mark of her presence in the passage of the story. Brajeshwar, of course, has been shown as a devoted son prepared to overlook the most callous and unprincipled conduct of his father under the ruse that one's father should be revered as someone more exalted than all the gods in heaven. At his instance Brajeshwar deserted his wife and this was perhaps a blessing because the Prafulla who came back to him was not quite the one who had been thrown out of his house. The vulnerable, abandoned wife got transformed into an assertive, self-confident individual, the legendary Debichoudhurani.

Chokher Bali (1903)

Tagore's *Chokher Bali* is perhaps the first Bengali novel with a distinct psychological undercurrent marking out different characters as well as the central theme. The actions and interactions involving the four major characters in the drama, the clashes of interests and conflicts shed new light on man-woman relationships and highlights the significance of interpersonal relationships in the evolution and exploration of the intricacies and complexities of human behaviour. The story starts on a placid note as we are introduced to Mahendra and Asha, an ideal couple very much in love with each other, whiling away their time in an idyllic situation sustained and supported by an indulgent mother and an aunt, and a very understanding and loyal friend. Then Binodini arrived on the scene, the beautiful, accomplished and competent young woman to cast a shadow on this allround atmosphere of happiness. Binodini carried within her a hidden seed of hostility and envy to Asha, Mahendra's wife. She tried to entice and entrap Mahendra and take her revenge on Asha. Asha, she thought was responsible for depriving her of her life's happiness, as Mahendra decided to marry Asha after spurning the proposal of marriage with her. Binodini's first objective was to create a rift between him and Asha and prove herself a woman much superior to Asha in every respect. Fickle-minded and egotistic Mahendra offered her ample opportunities to project that impression. Behari, Mahendra's friend, tried to intervene in the disaster brewing around the couple from a distance. He had always been a silent admirer of Asha and was determined not to let Binodini destroy this simple, innocent girl. Binodini in the meantime became familiar with Behari and discovered in him a man with rare qualities of sensitivity, understanding and reticence and felt strongly attracted to him. Behari's initial indifference also turned into a sympathetic interest in her affairs and her welfare as well. Binodini could not have expected anything more from life. Gently refusing to accept Behari's marriage proposal, she withdrew herself and decided to lead an existence away from all the turbulence and temptations of life.

Gora (1910)

In *Gora*, Tagore intended the story-line to develop on two different planes reflecting the aspirations and goals of a nation in transition and presenting complex human relationships against this background. At one level we find Gora as the representative of the burgeoning feelings and awakening of nationalism and with it he compared his faith in the concept of religious revivalism. At the other level was the question of interpersonal relationships involving other major characters of the novel, Benoy, Anandamayee, Sucharita, Lalita and others. For Gora the ultimate salvation of his dependent country lay in the strict adherence to age-old traditions laid down by Hindu orthodox society. He viewed it as a weapon to assert one's self-identity and the distinct identity of the nation. Any departure from this Gora perceived as a betrayal of the cause of his beloved motherland. Precisely because of that he was highly critical of the Brahmo society as a breakaway group of the Hindus. He was no less critical of the Brahmo women as he accused them of willingly forsaking the ideals of Hindu womanhood and aping the Western model rather mindlessly. He was also scathingly sarcastic about his friend Benoy's supposed infatuation with two Brahmo girls, Sucharita and Lalita, and to Paresh Babu's household. But Sucharita's serene demeanour, her intelligent understanding had a very unsettling effect on Gora. He could not deny, at least to himself, a sneaking admiration for the quite competent young woman. On the other side was the mother, Anandamayee, steadfastly refusing to subscribe to Gora's orthodox *Hindutva* and upholding her message of the universality of human beings. Anandamayee's contention in this context was very clear. Once she had accepted and welcomed Gora as her son, she could not have pretended to adhere to the orthodox society's injunctions. The secret of Gora's birth was a mystery shared only by Anandamayee and her husband, although the author chose to divulge it to the readers quite early at the onset of the story. Gora, in reality, was the son of a European couple who had died during the 'Sepoy Mutiny' and Gora was adopted by Anandamayee and her husband. The secret of Gora's real parentage when disclosed to him presented an ironic twist to his life and his world-view. Now, face to face with the reality he realized how correct both Anandamayee and Paresh Babu's vision of life, religion, nation and humanity was. In the end he accepted Paresh Babu, not quite conventional and indoctrinated a Brahmo, as his guru and in his mother's tolerant and compassionate nature could discover the true image of his country.

Ghare Baire (1915)

Ghaire Baire is a story of clashes and conflicts, both emotional and psychological, between three major characters, one woman and two men. Bimala and Nikhilesh were a happily married couple until the time when Sandeep, a revolutionary activist and

Nikhilesh's friend, appeared on the scene. Nikhilesh, educated and enlightened, wanted his wife Bimala, to come out of her secluded existence and to realize her real worth, and in the process to be able to know the real worth of the man she had married. Quite naturally, when Sandeep came to Nikhilesh's *zamindari*, and made his friend's house his headquarters for carrying on his political activities, Nikhilesh introduced his wife to him. Sandeep, an extrovert by nature, rather demonstrative of his emotions, took no time to strike a special friendship with Bimala. First, he profitably used his background as a political activist and a freedom-fighter and then he started extolling her potential as a sympathizer and an actual campaigner of his kind of politics. Gradually, his supposedly objective observations about service to the country and the vital roles women can play in this sphere took a personal turn-around and Sandeep managed to produce a mesmerizing impact on Bimala's body and soul. Nikhilesh could not do anything but be a silent spectator as he always wanted to give his wife full freedom to establish herself as an independent individual. He did not want to appear to be interfering with his wife's affairs. The rift was widening, and it was Nikhilesh's elder sister-in-law, out of her affectionate consideration for him, who warned him against the imminent breakdown of the relationship. The climax came with Bimala's own realization of Sandeep's real character. The power hungry and avaricious in his nature completely overshadowed whatever was noble and worthwhile in it. But, by that time, the final damage had been done. Sandeep's misconceived actions were about to erupt in a communal conflict among Nikhilesh's subjects and it was he who went out to quell the fire. The story ends on a note of suspense, the news of Nikhilesh's grievous injury and the uncertainty of his survival floating up to Bimala's conscience stricken, feverish self.

Jogajog (1929)

Initially the story centres around a family feud—conflicts of interests, of culture, of tradition between two hostile groups—one representing the values of the aristocratic land-owning elite family, with declining glory, and the other a new rich, mercantile business house. Madhusudan, the chief actor in this drama, was a successful businessman. Crude and masterful, with recently acquired wealth, he wanted to enter into a marriage alliance with the other family. This way, he thought, he would be able to put a final stamp of his victory in this ongoing clash. Bipradas, the eldest of the other family, was wary about the outcome of this match, but his sister Kumudini, in her trusting innocence, considered it a divine intervention and a way out of the family's dire financial straits. She had always entertained and cherished an idealized image of a husband, understanding, loving and compassionate. The reality could not have been any further from the picture she sustained in her mind. Madhusudan's boorish boastfulness and vulgar display of power created a sense of revulsion which all her desperate efforts could not wipe out from her mind. Kumudini very soon realized however she might try, she could not make their marriage work. By nature, inclinations and upbringing, they were poles apart and marital incompatibility assumed a proportion that was impossible to overcome. Kumudini came back to her brother. Bipradas could never have entertained the idea of sending her back to her husband's home where she would have to compromise her self-respect and sense of values. Then came the revelation which changed the colour of the whole situation. Kumudini's impending motherhood posed a problem which had to be resolved. Bipradas could not deprive Kumu's unborn child of its rightful parentage. Kumu once again prepared to go back to her husband, but this time with an optimistic note that she would come back once she had raised her child and done her duty to her husband's family.

Palli Samaj (Village Society) (1916)

Palli Samaj is a conglomeration of different characters with widely varying interests and concerns interacting with one another. Beni is the representative of the vested interests in maintaining the status quo in the village society and out to reap profit from the less fortunate members of the narrow and superstitious village society. Ramesh, after a long absence, came back to the village and was determined to root out the injustice inherent in the system and put a stop to the evil practices perpetuated by the more powerful section of society. Consequently there erupted a clash of interests. Bishweshwari, Beni's mother, tried to strike a balance between the conflicting aspirations of the two cousins, but her sympathy was always with Ramesh, not her own son. Rama was trapped in the cesspool of controversy and she had to side with Beni even against her own wishes. Rama always had a silent admiration and affection for Ramesh and Ramesh also reciprocated her feelings. But there remained the insurmountable barriers in between—the social barriers as society could never approve of any relation of a widow with another man, and the barrier which was erected because of their conflicting claims over property matters. Bishweshwari could empathize with Rama but could not find a way out of the emotional impasse she was in. In the end, she decided to take Rama along with her to a place of pilgrimage where, she thought, Rama could at least live in peace with herself and the world around her.

Arakshania (1916)

Arakshania is the story of a helpless widowed mother and her young unmarried daughter, Gyanada. Gyanada's mother's lack of resources and the daughter's lack of physical attributes make a suitable marriage for the girl an impossible proposition. Gyanada's mother tried to shield her daughter as long as possible against societal pressure. Orthodox Hindu tradition would not allow a girl to remain unmarried after a certain age, after she attains puberty as she becomes an *arakshania*—one who could not be protected any longer. But gradually the mother's patience also wears out and she gives vent to all her frustrated anger by taking it out on the unfortunate girl. She, after a prolonged illness, dies with her unfulfilled dream of seeing her daughter married and settled in life. In the end Atul, Gyanada's aunt's nephew who had once entertained some tender feelings for her, decided to come to her rescue and marry her and this brings the story somewhat to a happy end.

Shrikanta (1917-1933)

Shrikanta, in four parts, spread over a period of nearly sixteen years (1917-33) is more a saga of a wayfarer than a close-knit novel. In all four parts, Shrikanta plays the pivotal role and other characters move around this central figure—appearing at some particular point of his life and then fading out. Rajlakshmi is the only one among the dramatis personae who has a hold over the development of the story. She is the only thread perpetually woven around the whole life story of Shrikanta. In the first part, when Shrikanta was a young boy, he came in contact with a remarkable character, Annadadidi. This chance encounter had a lasting effect on moulding his attitude towards women and society's treatment of them. Towards the end of this part we have been introduced to Rajlakshmi in her Piary Baiji incarnation. In her Shrikanta discovered his long lost friend and companion of childhood days. Later he had to take shelter in Rajlakshmi's house in Patna and was acquainted with Rajlakshmi's step son Banku and her present preoccupation as the mother of her stepchildren and an affluent householder. Shrikanta left Patna with the precious knowledge of Rajlakshmi's unchanging love for him and the realization that sublime love not only attracts one closer to ones beloved, but has the power, too, to create a distance, if necessary, between the two and at the same time keep the relationship intact.

In the second part of the novel, the most important event happens to be Shrikanta's journey to Myanmar in search of a job and his introduction to another remarkable woman, Abhaya. Abhaya came to Myanmar in search of her husband who was working there and had taken a Burmese wife and had children too. Rohini, a distant cousin of Abhaya, escorted her to Myanmar and clearly entertained a soft feeling for her. When Abhaya a failed to create an honourable place for herself in her husband's life and home, she decided to spend the rest of her life with Rohini who had sacrificed and left behind all the prospects and possibilities of life for her sake. She knew that the orthodox society would not perceive this union as a legitimate one, but that did not deter her from taking this bold decision. She would rather stay outside the mainstream society and try to make a worthwhile beginning of her new life. Abhaya's example rekindled Rajlakshmi's expectations of investing her association with Shrikanta with a legal status. But once again it was Shrikanta who retreated. After this incident, a change came over in Rajlakshmi's attitude towards Shrikanta and the sort of life she was sharing with him. The inherent futility of this relationship appeared to have hit her more forcefully now than ever before and she tried, with a show of indifference, to keep her distance from Shrikanta.

The third part of the novel is devoted to Rajlakshmi and Shrikanta's life in a small village, Gangamati, where the reader encounters a number of minor characters without much of a development in the Rajlakshmi-Srikanta relationship or taking the story appreciably further on. The major portion of the fourth part revolves around two characters, Gahar, Shrikanta's childhood friend and Kamal Lata, a devotee of the Vaishnava cult. Both these episodes are quite loose ended without having much bearing on the theme of the story. This part ends rather abruptly with Kamal Lata's departure for Vrindavan and Shrikanta's tearful farewell to her.

Debdas (1917)

Debdas and Parbati from their childhood grew up together. Their adolescent attachment and affection took deep roots, at least in the mind of Parbati. When she came of age, and it was time for her marriage, she could not think of any one other than Debdas as her husband. Debdas was initially indecisive and the realization of his love for Parbati came a little too late. By that time, she was married off to a man much older in age. Parbati accepted her fate with apparent equanimity, and started acting out her role as a devoted wife and affectionate mother to her grown up stepchildren. Debdas always lacked Parbati's maturity and tried to drown his sorrows in drinking and an absolutely rudderless existence, steeped in what would conventionally be termed as debauchery. One of these vices was visiting a courtesan. In his case, Chandramukhi, the courtesan, turned out to be a woman of exceptional qualities, who gave up her successful profession and plush life for his sake, without expecting any return from him. Debdas also could not think of giving her any meaningful position or recognition in his life. After a graphic description of Debdas's complete dissipation, the story ends with his death almost at Parbati's doorstep.

Charitraheen (1917)

Charitraheen starts as a story of Satish and Savitri, their mutual interaction and gradual development of a distinct relationship. Satish is a student of a medical school in Calcutta and stays in a boarding house and Savitri was a widow in the boarding house, her position was somewhat of a housekeeper. Very soon they started a relationship of joking, teasing and bantering repartees. At one point, when Savitri realized that their innocent interchanges were about to take a serious turn and on Satish's part it was turning out to be an infatuation, she decided to withdraw herself completely from Satish's life. She knew that their relationship had no future, as society would treat her as nothing but a fallen woman, and she accepted self-exile. She intentionally left behind an impression that she was going to live-in with another man so that it would be easier for Satish to get over his involvement with her. Savitri's redemption came when was accepted and recognized as the honest, upright and moralistic Upendra's 'sister' and his companion during the last few days of his life. Side by side with the episode of Satish and Savitri, there is another episode running which involves Satish, Upendra, Kiranmayee and Upendra's wife Surobala, albeit indirectly. Kiranmayee, Upendra's ailing friend's wife, remains all along an enigma. Her incomparable beauty along with her razor-sharp intelligence and unconventional attitude and behaviour made her a truly remarkable character. Life did not have much to offer to her except for her husband's supreme indifference to her physical and emotional needs and an opportunistic mother-in-law's insensitive treatment. Her mother-in-law not only turned a blind eye to her affair with the family doctor; rather, she encouraged her to carry on with him. All these things together managed to turn her into a hard hearted cynic. And then appeared Upendra with Satish to visit his critically ill friend.

Kiranmayee could discover in him the 'ideal' man and the 'ideal' husband and was reminded of the complete void that was her lot and life.

After her husband's death she did not hesitate for a moment to express her true feelings towards this new man in her life. Upendra was an understanding man. In spite of his single-minded devotion to his wife, Surobala, he was prepared to make some concessions to this young and intelligent widow and decided to put Dibakar, his cousin, under her guardianship for his college education. But, later some negligence on Dibakar's part and some lapses of Kiranmayee's enraged Upendra. He not only severely reprimanded Dibakar and asked him to leave the place immediately, but hinted at Kiranmayee's unseemly conduct and behaviour with the young boy. In the frenzy of her anger, Kiranmayee decided to elope with Dibakar and during the same night managed to sail to Burma. After a few months' sordid existence and Kiranmayee's incessant struggle for an honourable survival there, Satish arrived with the news of Upendra's terminal illness. His insistence forced Kiranmayee to accompany him to Calcutta along with Dibakar. The novel ends with Upendra's death and Kiranmayee's eventual loss of sanity.

Gribadaba (1920)

The story line in *Gribadaba* revolves around Achala and her divided loyalty to two different men—Mahim and Suresh. Achala was torn between two conflicting emotions, her inherent trust in Mahim's solid, rock-like steadfastness and her attraction towards Suresh's impetuous, ever so transparent protestation of love and loyalty. Achala tried to get over what she thought was her infatuation with Suresh by accepting Mahim as her husband. But after their marriage things came to an unfortunate pass instead of getting settled down. With the arrival of Suresh at Mahim's unpretentious village home, the situation took a precarious turn. Achala's obvious disillusionment with village life and the ideal picture of blissful married life helped Suresh come to the conclusion that their marriage was not working out as it should have. This realization gave impetus to his expectation of a renewed relationship with Achala. This along with his miscalculation that Achala's love for him had remained unaffected, drove him to take the desperate decision to separate Achala from her ailing husband in the running train. But once they were in Dihri and were forced to keep up the pretence of a husband-wife relationship, a peculiar void, an all-pervasive emptiness engulfed his life. Achala could never come to terms with the life she was leading with Suresh and Suresh himself was getting rather tired of the futility of the whole existence. His death came as a welcome escape from the agony that was his life.

The character of Mrinal has been presented in the novel as an antithesis to Achala. She symbolizes everything that has been perceived as the essential attribute of ideal womanhood. Her sense of chastity, her unwavering devotion to her husband, her selfless service to others, all together raised her to the pedestal of a preceptor, and she was the one who could at the end predict with supreme confidence the possibilities that lay in store in Achala's future.

Bamuner Meye (1920)

Bamuner Meye once again is a story of an orthodox, tradition-bound village society and meaningless adherence to age-old superstitious practices. Sandhya, daughter of a Kulin Brahmin family is of marriageable age and is quite friendly with Arun, who was a Brahmin but of a lower rank. And when he expressed the desire to marry her, Sandhya could not rise above her family pride and pedigree and refused to accept his proposal. Very soon her marriage to a Kulin Brahmin was fixed and her grandmother, who used to live in Varanasi as a social recluse, arrived to attend her only granddaughter's wedding. This lady was one of the several wives of her Kulin husband and after her husband's death she shifted to Varanasi with her only son. Before Sandhya's marriage could be solemnized, the secret behind the old lady's reclusive life came to light. Sandhya's father was not the son of his Kulin father. This Kulin Brahmin in his old age deputed a barber to impersonate him and visit his innumerable, unknown wives and used to share the money extracted from his wives' fathers; Sandhya's father was the offspring of this barber. After this disclosure the bridegroom's party left in a huff and Sandhya rushed to Arun with an appeal to rescue her. Arun was initially hesitant and Sandhya decided to seek out an existence outside the rigid framework of marriage and the socially prescribed role of a married woman and left the village with her father for Vrindavan.

Bibliography

Allen, Michael and S.N. Mukherjee, eds., *Women in India and Nepal*, Canberra: ANU, 1982.

Altekar, A.S., *The Position of Women in Hindu Civilisation*, New Delhi: Motilal Banarasidass, 3rd edn., 1962.

Anjum, Mohini, ed., *Muslim Women in India*, New Delhi: Radiant Publishers, 1992.

Ardener, Sherley, ed., *Women and Space: Ground Rules and Social Maps*, London: Croom Helm, 1981.

Bandhopadhyaya, Shreekumar, *Banga Sahitye Upanyaser Dhara*, Calcutta: Modern Book Agency, rpt., 1984.

Banerjee, Srikumar, 'Rabindranath's Novels', in B.M. Choudhury, ed., *Homage to Rabindranath Tagore*, Kharagpur: IIT, 1961.

Banton, Michael, *Roles: An Introduction to the Study of Social Relations*, London: Tavistock Publications, 1965.

de Beauvoir, Simone, *The Second Sex*, tr. H.M. Parshley, London: Picador, 1988.

Beetham, David, *The Legitimation of Power*, London: Macmillan Education Ltd., 1991.

Bernstein, Gail Lee, ed., *Recreating Japanese Women, 1600-1945*, Berkeley, Los Angeles, Oxford: University of California Press, 1991.

Beteille, André and T.N. Madan, eds., *Encounter and Experience*, New Delhi: Vikas, 1975.

Biswas, Dipti Kumar, *Sociology of Major Bengali Novels*, Gurgaon: The Academic Press, 1974.

Borthwick, Meredith, *The Changing Role of Women in Bengal, 1849-1905*, Princeton: Princeton University Press, 1984.

Bose, Buddhadev, *An Acre of Green Grass*, Calcutta: Papyrus, rpt., 1982.

Bose, S.C., *Hindoos As They Are: A Description of Manners, Customs and Inner Life of Hindoo Society in Bengal*, Calcutta, 1881.

Chakravarty, Usha, *Condition of Bengali Women*, Calcutta: Firma K.L. Mukhopadhyaya, 1963.

Collet, Sophia Dobson, *The Life and Letters of Raja Rammohun Roy*, eds. D.K. Biswas and P.C. Ganguly, Calcutta: Sadharan Brahmo Samaj, 1962.

Chanana, Karuna, ed., *Socialization, Education and Women*, New Delhi: Orient Longman, 1988.

Chandra, Sudhir, *The Oppressive Present: Literature and Social Consciousness in Colonial India*, New Delhi: OUP, 1994.

———, 'Enslaved Daughters: Nationalism, Law and Women's Rights', New Delhi: OUP, 1999.

The following are from *Bankim Rachnavali* (A Collection of Bankimchandra Chatterjee's Novels), vol. I, ed. Yogesh Chandra Bagal, Calcutta: Sahitya Samsad, 1990.

——*Indira* (1873)

——*Bishvabriksha* (1873)

——*Krishnakanter Will* (1878)

——*Debichoudhurani* (1884)

The following are from *Sarat Rachnavali* (A Collection of Sarat Chandra Chatterjee's Novels), vol. I, Calcutta: Tuli Kalam, 1989.

——*Biraj Bau* (1914)

——*Parineeta* (1914)

——*Palli Samaj* (1916)

——*Arakshania* (1916)

——*Shrikanta* (Four Parts) (1917-33)

——*Narir Mulya*, (essay), vol. II (1924)

——*Debdas* (1917)

——*Charitraheen* (1917)

——*Datta*

——*Gribadaha* (1920)

——*Bamuner Meye* (1920)

——*Patherdabi* (1926)

——*Sheshprashna* (1931)

——*Bipradas* (1935)

Chatterjee, Joya, *Bengal Divided: Hindu Communalism and Partition, 1932-1947*, Cambridge University Press, 1999.

Chatterjee, Partha, *The Nation and its Fragments: Colonial and Post-Colonial History*, New Delhi: OUP, 1995.

Cott, Nancy F., *The Bonds of Womanhood: Woman's Sphere in New England, 1780-1835*, New Haven and London: Yale University Press, 1977.

Das, S., *Purdah: The Status of Indian Women*, New Delhi: Ess Ess Publication, 1979.

Dhruvarajan, Vanaja, *Hindu Women and the Power of Ideology*, New Delhi: Vistaar Publication, 1989.

Deb, Chitra, *Thakur Barir Andar Mahal*, Calcutta: Ananda Publishers, n.d.

Debichoudhurani, Indira, *Puratani*, Calcutta, n.d.

Debichoudhurani, Sarala, *Jibaner Jharapata*, Calcutta: Rupa, n.d.

Desai, Neera and Maithreyee Krishnaraj, *Women and Society in India*, Delhi: Ajanta Publication, 1987.

Dube, Leela, Eleanor Leacock and Shirley Ardener, eds., *Visibility and Power: Essays on Women in Society and Development*, New Delhi: OUP, 1986.

———, 'Women's World: Three Encounters', in A. Beteille and T.N. Madan, eds., *Encounter and Experience*, New Delhi: Vikas, 1975.

Giddens, Anthony, *Modernity and Self-Identity: Self and Society in the Late Modern Age*, Cambridge, U.S.: Polity Press, 1991.

Gilbert, Sandra M. and Susan Gubar, *No Man's Land: The Place of The Woman Writer in the Twentieth Century, vol. I, The War of The Words*, New Haven and London: Yale University Press, 1988.

Goffman, Erving, *The Presentation of Self in Everyday Life*, New York: Doubleday Anchor Books, 1959.

———, *Asylums*, New Delhi: Penguin, 1968.

Good, William J., *The Family*, Delhi: Prentice-Hall, 1987.

Gorham, Debora, *The Victorian Girl and The Feminine Ideal*, London and Canberra: Croom Helm, 1982.

Ghoshjaya, Kumudini, *Bidhava Vivaha*, Calcutta, 1925.

Hatcher, A. Brain, *Idioms of Improvement: Vidyasagar and Cultural Encounter in Bengal*, New Delhi: Oxford India Paperbacks, OUP, 2000.

Inden, Ronald B., *Marriage and Rank in Bengali Culture*, New Delhi: Vikas, 1976.

Jacobson, D. and S.S. Wadley, *Women in India: Two Perspectives*, New Delhi, Manohar, 1977.

Jain, Pratibha and Rajan Mahan, eds., *Women Images*, Jaipur: Rewat Publications, 1996.

Jayawardena, Kumari, *Feminism and Nationalism in the Third World*, New Delhi: Kali for Women, 1986.

Jeffery, Patricia, *Frogs in a Well: Indian Women in Purdah*, New Delhi: Manohar, rpt. 1999.

Jain, Ravindra K., ed., *Text and Context: The Social Anthropology of Tradition*, vol. II, Philadelphia: ISHI, 1977.

Joardar, B., *Prostitution in Nineteenth and Early Twentieth Century Calcutta,* New Delhi: Inter-India Publications, 1985.

Joshi, V.C., ed., *Rammohun Roy and the Process of Modernization in India*, New Delhi: Vikas, 1975.

Kabir, Humayun, *The Bengali Novel*, Calcutta: Firma K.L. Mukhopadhyaya, 1968.

———, *Sarat Chandra Chatterjee*, Calcutta: Silpee Sangstha Prakasani, 1963.

Kakar, Sudhir, ed., *Identity and Adulthood*, New Delhi: OUP, 1982.

Kakar, Sudhir, *Intimate Relations: Exploring Indian Sexuality*, New Delhi: Penguin, rpt., 1989.

———, *The Inner World: A Psycho-analytic Study of Childhood and Society in India*, 2nd edn., New Delhi: OUP, 1992.

Kapadia, K.M., *Marriage and Family in India*, New Delhi, OUP.

Karlekar, Malavika, *Voices From Within: Early Personal Narratives of Bengali Women*, New Delhi: OUP, 1991.

Klapisch-Zuber, Christiane, ed., *Silences of the Middle Ages*, vol. II of *A History of Women in the West*, Georges Duby and Michelle Perrot, general eds., The Bellknap Press, Harvard University Press, 1992.

Ko, Dorothy, *Teachers of the Inner Chamber: Women and Culture in 17th Century China*, Stanford: Stanford University Press, 1994.

Koehler, Lyle, *A Search for Power: 'The Weaker Sex' in Seventeenth Century, New England*, Urbana, Chicago, London: University of Illinois Press, 1980.

Kopf, David, *The Brahmo Samaj and Shaping of the Modern Indian Mind*, Princeton: Princeton University Press, 1979.

———, *British Orientalism and Bengal Renaissance*, Berkeley: University of California Press, 1969.

Majumdar, B.B., *Heroines of Tagore: A Study in the Transformation of Indian Society 1875-1941*, Calcutta: Firma K.L. Mukhopadhyaya, 1968.

Mazumdar, Sudha (ed. Geraldine, H. Forbes), *A Pattern of Life: The Memoirs of an Indian Woman*, New Delhi: Manohar, 1977.

McGuire, John, *The Making of a Colonial Mind: A Quantitative Study of the Bhadralok in Calcutta, 1857-1885*, Canberra: ANU, 1983.

Menon, K.P.K., *Tagore Lecture 1973*, Tamil Nadu: Annamalai University, 1976.

Merton, Robert K., *Social Theory and Social Structure*, enlarged edn., New York: Free Press, 1968.

———, *Sociological Ambivalence and Other Essays*, New York: The Free Press, 1976.

Mies, Maria, *Indian Women and Patriarchy: Conflicts and Dilemmas of Students and Working Women*, New Delhi: Concept Publishing Company, 1980.

Mukherjee, Meenakshi, *Realism and Reality: The Novel and Society in India*, New Delhi: OUP, 1985.

Mukherjee, Prabhati, *Hindu Women: Normative Models*, New Delhi: Orient Longman, 1978.

Mukherjee, Sujit, *Towards a Literary History of India*, Simla: IIAS, 1975.

Murshid, Ghulam, *Reluctant Debutante: Response of Bengali Women to Modernization, 1849-1905*, Rajshahi: Sahitya Samsad, Rajshahi University, 1983.

Nadel, S.F., *The Theory of Social Structure*, London: Cohen and West, 1957.

Nag, K. and D. Burman, eds., *Selected Works of Raja Rammohun Roy*, New Delhi: Govt. of India Publications, 1977.

Nanda, B.R., ed., *Indian Women: From Purdah to Modernity*, New Delhi: Vikas, 1976.

Nead, Lynda, *Myths of Sexuality: Representation of Women in Victorian Britain*, Oxford: Basil Blackwell, 1988.

Nestor, Pauline, *Female Friendships and Communities*, Oxford: Clarendon Press, 1985.

Ostor, Akos, Leena Fruzzetti and Steve Barnet, eds., *Concepts of Person: Kinship, Caste and Marriage in India*, New Delhi: OUP, 1992.

Perrot, Michelle, ed., *Writing Women's History*, Oxford: Basil Blackwell, 1992.

Poddar, Arabinda, *Renaissance in Bengal: Quest and Confrontation 1800-1860*, Simla: IIAS, 1970.

———, *Renaissance in Bengal: Search for Identity*, Simla: IIAS, 1977.

Raj, Sebasti L., S.J., *Quest for Gender Justice: A Critique of the Status of Women in India*, Madras: T.R. Publication, 1991.

Raj, G.V., *Tagore, the Novelist*, New Delhi: Sterling, 1983.

Ray, Rajat K., 'Man, Woman and the Novel: The Rise of a New Consciousness in Bengal, 1858-1947', *The Indian Economic and Social History Review*, XVI: I, 1979.

———, *Mind, Body and Society: Life, and Mentality in Colonial Bengal*, Calcutta: OUP, 1995.

Raychaudhury, Tapan, *Europe Reconsidered*, New Delhi: OUP, 1988.

Risley, H.H., *Tribes and Castes of Bengal*, 2 vols., Calcutta: Secretariat Press, rpt., 1991-2.

Rosaldo, M.Z. and L. Lamphere, *Woman, Culture and Society*, Stanford: Stanford University Press, 1974.

Roy, Bharati, ed., *From the Seams of History: Essays on Indian Women*, New Delhi: Oxford India Paperbacks, OUP, 1997.

Roy, Manisha, *Bengali Women*, Chicago: University of Chicago Press, 1975.

Sangari, Kumkum and Sudesh Vaid, eds., *Recasting Women: Essays in Colonial History*, New Delhi: Kali for Women, 1988.

———, *Women and Culture*, Bombay: SNDT University, 1985.

Sarada, M., *Rabindranath Tagore: A Study of Women Characters in his Novels*, New Delhi: Sterling, 1988.

Sarkar, Sumit, *Swadesh Movement in Bengal, 1903-1908*, New Delhi: PPH, 1973.

———, *Modern India, 1885-1947*, New Delhi: Macmillan India, 1983.

———, *A Critique of Colonial India*, Calcutta: Papyrus, 1985.

Sarkar, S.C., *Bengal Renaissance and Other Essays*, New Delhi: PPH, 1970.

Sen, Amiya P., *Hindu Revivalism in Bengal, 1872-1905: Some Essays in Interpretation*, New Delhi: Oxford India Paperbacks, OUP, 1993.

Sen, Asok, *Vidyasagar and His Elusive Milestones*, Calcutta: Ridhi-India, 1977.

Sengupta, Padmini, *Women in India*, New Delhi: Information Service of India, n.d.

Sengupta, S., *Study of the Women of Bengal*, Calcutta: Indian Publication, 1970.

Sharoni, Simona, 'Every Woman is an Occupied Territory: The Politics of Militarism and Sexism and the Israeli-Palestinian Conflict', *Journal of Gender Studies*, vol. I, 4, Nov. 1992, pp. 447-62.

Sinha, Pradip, *Nineteenth-Century Bengal: Aspects of Social History*, Calcutta: Firma K.L. Mukhopadhyaya, 1975.

Stimpson, Catherine R. and Ethel Spector Parson, eds., *Women, Sex and Sexuality*, Chicago and London: University of Chicago Press, 1980.

Sutherland, Sally J.M., ed., *Bridging Worlds: Studies on Women in South-Asia*, Oxford: OUP, 1991.

Tagore, Rabindranath, *Rabindra Rachanavali*, vol. VII (short stories), Calcutta: West Bengal Govt. Publications, 1961.

———, *Chokher Bali* (1903), Centenary edn., vol. VIII.

———, *Gora* (1909), ibid., vol. IX.

———, *Ghare Baire* (1916), Vishva Bharati edn., vol. IV, 1987.

———, *Jogajog* (1926), Centenary edn., vol. IX.

Thapan, Meenakshi, ed., *Embodiment: Essays on Gender and Identity*, New Delhi: OUP, 1997.

Urqurhart, Margaret M., *Women of Bengal*, Calcutta: Association Press, 1927.

Vicinus, Martha, ed., *A Widening Sphere: Changing Roles of Victorian Women*, London: Methuen, 1980.

Vijaylakshmi, *Sex Role Perception and Occupational Choice*, New Delhi: Mittal Publication, 1989.

Watson, Rubie S. and P.B. Ebrey, eds., *Marriage and Inequality in Chinese Society*, Berkeley, Los Angeles, Oxford: University of California Press, 1991.

MANUSCRIPTS AND PRIVATE PAPERS

At the Oriental and India Office Collections, the British Library (formerly The India Office Library and Records), London:

'Women in Bengal: Papers of Sir Herbert Risley, 1901-1911' (Risley Collections: MSS. Eur. E 295/19)

'Education of Women: Memoirs of Florence Marya Wyld'

'Annette Akroyd-Beveridge Collection: Diary and Note Book in India, (1872-78)'

PRINTED DOCUMENTS

At the Oriental and India Office Collections, the British Library (formerly the India Office Library and Records), London:

Tracts (*European Languages*)

Ghoshal, Sarla Devi, 'A Scheme for an Indian Girl School', vol. 923.
Gupta, L.C.D., 'An Essay on Hindu Joint Family', vol. 941.
———, 'Widow-Remarriage', ibid.
Sen, K.C., 'The Improvement of Indian Women', vol. 946.

Tracts (*Vernacular*)

Basu, Rajnarayan, 'Sekal ar Ekal'.
Gupta, Jyotinchandra, 'Hindu Narir Kartavya'.
Gupta, Prasannatara, 'Parivarik Jivan'.

Index